TWAYNE'S WORLD AUTHORS SERIES

A Survey of the World's Literature

Sylvia E. Bowman, Indiana University

GENERAL EDITOR

SPAIN

Janet W. Díaz, University of North Carolina at Chapel Hill
Gerald E. Wade, Vanderbilt University

EDITORS

Ramón de Mesonero Romanos

TWAS 385

Ramón de Mesonero Romanos

RAMÓN DE MESONERO ROMANOS

By RICHARD A. CURRY
University of Nevada, Reno

TWAYNE PUBLISHERS
A DIVISION OF G. K. HALL & CO., BOSTON

Library of Congress Cataloging in Publication Data

Curry, Richard A   1939–
    Ramón de Mesonero Romanos

    (Twayne's world authors series; TWAS 385: Spain)
    Bibliography: pp. 167–76.
    Includes index.
    1.   Mesonero y Romanos, Ramón de, 1803–1882.
PQ6539.Z5C8   868'.5'09   76–25
ISBN 0–8057–6226–4

To my mother and father

Contents

About the Author

Professor Richard A. Curry was born on March 31, 1939 in Seattle, Washington. He graduated from the University of Washington in 1964, receiving Magna Cum Laude and Phi Beta Kappa honors. During these years of study toward the B.A., he lived and studied in Spanish-speaking areas for two years. Professor Curry spent the period of 1964–66 teaching at the high school and community college level, returning to the University of Washington for graduate studies in 1966. His M.A. in Spanish literature was granted in 1967, and his Ph.D. in the same field in 1971. His dissertation dealt with the novelistic art of Benito Pérez Galdós. While pursuing the doctorate, he was the recipient of an NDEA Fellowship.

Professor Curry has served as Assistant Professor of Spanish at the University of California, Riverside; West Virginia University; and at the University of Georgia. He is now Associate Professor of Spanish at the University of Nevada, Reno. He has published several articles on Antonio Machado, a study on *Los amantes de Teruel*, and a book review on *El cerco* by Concha Lagos. Professor Curry has also delivered a paper on the techniques of characterization in the *costumbrista* sketches of Ramón de Mesonero Romanos. He is an active member of MLA, AATSP, ACTFL, and FLAG (Foreign Language Association of Georgia). At present he serves as chairman of the Committee on Awards for the National Spanish Contests of the AATSP.

Preface

The purpose of this study is to introduce the English-speaking reader to Ramón de Mesonero Romanos, the man and the writer. For many reasons it is understandable that all but the specialist in Spanish literature should be unaware of this name. Plagued by an inconsistent censorship, the confusion inherent in living in a period of rapid social and political transformation, and the lack of immediate or direct roots in periods of Spanish literary excellence, Mesonero Romanos and his contemporaries were unable to find the proper conditions for reasoned and free artistic creation. The mediocrity which some often associate with many middle class pursuits seems all too often—in an absolute sense—a defining trait of Spanish nineteenth-century literature before the novels of Pérez Galdós. One other obstacle to the fame of Don Ramón may be mentioned. His form—the sketch of manners—may rightfully be termed a minor genre. Its brevity, its ties to the commercial periodical press, and its hybrid nature (at the same time festive and ironic, entertaining and didactic) place great burdens on any author's ultimate esthetic aspirations.

In spite of these limitations, Mesonero made lasting contributions to the modernization of Spanish prose and to the establishment of Spanish Realism. Also, his importance in the development of Spanish journalism should not be overlooked. His newspaper sketches gave rise to a new interest in observation, in description, in local color and traditions, in the interplay of social and historical forces, and in a fresher, more direct, and less oratorical style. Although he preserved many characteristics from earlier Spanish literary tradition, Mesonero most definitely left his mark on the development of his country's letters. Overshadowed by Larra in some respects, he was certainly the most successful, influential, and imitated of the Spanish *costumbristas.* Today his name is nearly synonymous with this historically significant movement.

Within the obvious limitations of space, this book attempts to go beyond the boundaries of previous studies on Mesonero. That is, I attempt to give a relatively complete picture of the whole man and the entire gamut of his literary creation; at the same time, attention is given to details of style, form, and expression—especially as regards his *costumbrista* sketches. The dominant theme of any work on Mesonero must be his total commitment to and love for Madrid. While the sheer bulk and diversity of this author's work precludes analysis or even mention of every article, I do attempt to at least describe, if not analyze, each part of his work. Abridgements are necessary, especially with respect to articles on municipal betterment, civic history, biography, and literary criticism.

This book has no single thesis in a strict sense, but it does attempt to correct the frequently repeated portrait of Don Ramón as a smiling, backward-looking, bourgeois property owner who dabbled in comic articles. Mesonero is most definitely an eclectic; his independent literary voice is colored by his personality and by the weight of Spanish tradition, not by specific styles or movements. However, taking all of his works into account, I conclude and attempt to suggest that much of his energy is directed to the future, in a moral as well as a physical sense. That is, Don Ramón's articles are predominantly critical, rather than festive celebrations of things as they are or as they used to be. They try to promote awareness and improvement while they also amuse. Humor is normally (not always) used adroitly for control of narrator-reader relationships and in the service of the overall ironic intent; it is not usually the ultimate purpose of these sketches. Surprisingly, Mesonero's mordant comments at times rival those of his contemporary, Larra.

Due to the sheer weight of Don Ramón's works, I have chosen to organize my discussion of the *Escenas matritenses* (*Scenes of Madrid*) around basic characteristics of his themes, techniques, and style rather than to analyze an endless number of individual articles. I strive for detailed analysis whenever possible, but in many cases I have had to compromise with space limitations and only suggest the results of my previous analyses. Partially to remedy this difficulty, I have, in Chapter Five, translated

Preface

and analyzed one sketch especially selected for its representativeness rather than for ultimate esthetic superiority.

Because the material is widely known and readily available, I have not included a discussion of nineteenth-century history, except in brief references in Chapter One. The problem of literary sources is reviewed broadly in Chapter Two, but is not developed in detail with respect to specific articles. Several worthy studies are mentioned in the bibliography.

All translations within this study are mine; I have attempted to catch the flavor or texture of the prose rather than render a literal translation. Most quotations of Mesonero come from the five volume edition of his works found in the *Biblioteca de Autores Españoles* series. Reference is made to the volume and page number within the text. When citing from other editions, the items are documented in the Notes and References section. Also, many long titles are shortened after their initial complete reference. In pursuit of uniformity and in harmony with previous publications in English on Mesonero, I have decided to italicize the titles of the sketches rather than place them in quotation marks. This decision also has logic in that they were first conceived and published as individual units.

All modern scholarship on Mesonero owes a debt to Emilio Cotarelo y Mori. His influence, especially with regard to biography and bibliography, is significant within the following pages. My thanks also to Mrs. Becky Hooten, whose typing and proofreading helped speed this project to its conclusion.

RICHARD A. CURRY

University of Georgia

Chronology

1803 July 19: Ramón de Mesonero Romanos is born in Madrid.

1808– Receives direct, indelible impressions of the political in-
1814 stability, the foreign invasions, and the economic disaster
of these years. Already demonstrating a penetrating curiosity and a consciousness of history.

1820– Writes many poems, most of which he later renounced
1826 when he judged them uninspired.

1820 January 5: death of his father, Matías de Mesonero.
Ramón inherits the family's lucrative business interests,
and becomes, at age sixteen, the sole support of his family.

1821 Begins to write informal sketches of his classmates; these
writings remain unpublished.

1822 Publishes his first work, entitled *Mis ratos perdidos o
ligero bosquejo de Madrid en 1820 y 1821* (*My Free Time
or a Quick Outline of Madrid in 1820 and 1821*). José
María de Carnerero, editor of the newspaper *El Indicador
de las Novedades, de los Espectáculos y de las Artes*,
invites Mesonero to collaborate with him both as a writer
and as an editor. First article in May called *Tres días en
Aranjuez* (*Three Days at Aranjuez*). Mesonero continues
to write articles for various newspapers and magazines
on widely diverse topics.

1823 March 24: leaves for Seville and Cádiz as a member of
the constitutional government's militia.

1826 September: première of his first dramatic effort, a revision
of Tirso de Molina's *Amor por señas* (*To Love by Signs*),
which Mesonero called *Es una de las tres y de las tres no es
ninguna* (*It Is One of the Three and of the Three It Is
Not Anyone*). In December he stages another adaptation
of Tirso called *Ventura te dé Dios, hijo* (*May God Grant
Thee Fortune, Son*). Both were staged at the Príncipe
Theater.

1827 June 28: première at the Cruz Theater of adaptation of
Tirso's *La dama del olivar* (*The Lady from the Olive
Grove*) which Mesonero entitled *Lorenza la de Estercuel*.

In July he staged at the Cruz Theater a revision of Lope de Vega's *La viuda valenciana* (*The Valencian Widow*), preserving the original title.

1828   Revises Antonio Hurtado de Mendoza's *El marido hace mujer y el trato muda costumbre* (*Husbands Fashion Their Wives and Experience Changes Habits*), a play which Mesonero never staged. On November 25, his translation of M. de Mazères' *Marido joven y mujer vieja* (*A Young Husband and an Old Wife*) is staged at the Príncipe Theater.

1829   Composes his only original play, *La señora de protección y escuela de pretendientes* (*The Influence Peddler and Her School for Position Seekers*). This work was never produced, but served as inspiration for a later article *Pretender por alto* (*To Start at the Top*).

1830–   Mesonero is an active participant in the formation of
1831   one of the century's first formal literary societies, the *Parnasillo*.

1831   Publishes in October his first major work, *Manual de Madrid. Descripción de la corte y de la villa* (*Manual of Madrid. Description of the Court and the Town*). Revised editions appear in 1833, 1844, and 1854.

1832   January 12: Mesonero's first recognized article of customs, *El retrato* (*The Picture*), is published in *Cartas Españolas*.

1833–   Travels for nine months through France and England,
1834   making observations and comparisons directly influencing later civic writings and public service.

1834   July 19: Mesonero's mother, Teresa, dies of cholera while helping to cure her son of the same disease.

1835   January: publishes *Apéndice al "Manual de Madrid"* (*Appendix to the "Manual of Madrid"*). This reform-oriented work is a direct result of his European travels. Publishes *Panorama matritense* (*Panorama of Madrid*), his first collection of *costumbrista* articles. Plays a central role, as a member of the Economic Society of Madrid, in the organization of the *Ateneo*; becomes its first secretary. Takes control on May 1 of the newspaper *Diario de Madrid* and uses it as a vehicle for his articles on community betterment and social reform.

1836   April 3: founds and directs until 1842 *El Semanario Pintoresco Español.* Begins to publish his own sketches of manners in the *Semanario.* Secretary of the Fire Insurance Society. Librarian of the *Ateneo;* serves until 1839.

1837   Directly intervenes in the establishment of the *Liceo Artístico y Literario,* another significant outlet for new literary ideas.

1838   Named an honorary member of the Royal Spanish Academy on May 3, and pronounces his inaugural address on the Spanish novel on May 17. November 28: receives the Cross of Charles III.

1840–   Travels through Europe, especially in France and Bel-
1841   gium. Publishes *Recuerdos de viaje por Francia y Bélgica en 1840 y 1841 (Memoirs of a Journey Through France and Belgium in 1840 and 1841).*

1842   Publishes *Escenas matritenses (Scenes of Madrid),* a much expanded version of *Panorama matritense (Panorama of Madrid).* Major new editions follow in 1845 and 1851.

1843   Travels through southern and eastern Spain from April through October; personally witnesses certain events in another of Spain's political upheavals.

1846   Serves until 1849 as an elected member of the Madrid City Council. Intervenes in numerous projects for social advancement. Refuses the position of mayor. On May 23, he reads his lengthy *Proyecto de mejoras generales de Madrid (Plan for General Improvements in Madrid)* in a City Council session. Later the *Proyecto* was published. Named secretary of the Spanish Association of Property Owners.

1847   His *Ordenanzas de policía urbana y rural para la villa de Madrid y su término (Ordinances for the Public Welfare in Madrid)* is approved by the City Council and published. These regulations were law for many years. On February 25, he becomes a regular member of the Royal Spanish Academy.

1848   Publishes *Tirso de Molina. Cuentos, fábulas, descripciones, diálogos, máximas y apotegmas, epigramas y dichos agudos escogidos en sus obras (Tirso de Molina. Stories, Fables,*

Descriptions, Dialogues, Maxims and Epigrams Selected from His Works).

1849 June 27: marries Salomé de Ichaso.

1853– Director of the Madrid Savings Association.
1855

1857– Edits and writes introductory studies for five volumes
1861 in Rivadeneyra's *Biblioteca de Autores Españoles.*

1858 Named president of the Urban Sanitation Board. Serves as provincial deputy until 1859.

1861 Publishes *El antiguo Madrid (Ancient Madrid).*

1862 *Tipos, grupos y bocetos de cuadros de costumbres (Types, Groups and Outlines of Costumbrista Sketches),* a volume of new sketches written between 1843 and 1860 and published within a new edition called *Obras jocosas y satíricas del Curioso Parlante (Jocose and Satiric Works of the Curious Chatterbox).* This edition includes all of his previous *costumbrista* writings.

1864 July 15: named senior and official chronicler of Madrid.

1865– Intense effort via newspaper articles to stimulate improve-
1875 ments in modern Madrid as well as civic pride in the achievements of the past.

1871 May 18: receives the Great Cross of Isabel the Catholic.

1875 Publishes a catalogue of the holdings in his personal library.

1876 Named director of the Municipal Library.

1877 Publishes a catalogue of the holdings of the Municipal Library.

1880 Publishes *Memorias de un setentón (Memoirs of a Septuagenarian),* first as magazine articles and then in book form.

1881 Named lifetime director of the Municipal Library and chief of the city's archives. Becomes honorary lifetime director of the Property Owners Association.

1882 April 30: dies at age seventy-eight from a brain hemorrhage.

1883 His sons publish *Algo en prosa y en verso inédito (Some Unpublished Prose and Verse).*

1903– Mesonero's sons publish two volumes called *Trabajos*
1905 *no coleccionados (Uncollected Works).*

CHAPTER 1

Life and Writings: An Overview

AN enduring appreciation has been attached in Spain to the name Ramón de Mesonero Romanos. This has occurred principally because of the man's literary and civic achievements. Unlike others whose ties to a specific literary movement may cause periodic or permanent decline in popularity, Mesonero's eclecticism—ideological and stylistic—has produced a certain aura of timelessness around his life and works. All that he stands for seems to suggest solidity, common sense, and pragmatism. Mesonero may, however, seem exceptional in other ways for he was a man in the public domain who was keenly aware of his own limitations, who eschewed systematic pessimism or facile optimism, and who gave of himself freely, mostly without ulterior motive, in order to promote material and moral progress for his compatriots. In an era of political factionalism, his independent judgment and broad-based social works stand out clearly. Though not above normal human frailties and some pettiness, Mesonero's life and works, when studied, generally provide an uplifting experience.

I The Early Years

Ramón de Mesonero Romanos was born in Madrid on July 19, 1803. His birth took place at home at number 10 Olivo Street, a street renamed in 1883, one year after Mesonero's death, Calle de Mesonero Romanos. The second of five children, Mesonero was born to Don Matías Mesonero and Teresa Romanos, a couple who had lived in Madrid for twenty years. Don Matías was a native and always loyal Salamancan; he owned a prosperous business which provided Ramón with lasting security and influential acquaintances. Teresa, the author's mother, was from the region of Aragón; she is always

17

described by her son as virtuous, loving, and self-sacrificing. Later, she lost her life while nursing Ramón during an outbreak of cholera.

Mesonero's parents were somewhat conservative, fiercely patriotic, and religious to the letter of the law. Their home was a social center—a crossroads for local friends, old Salamancan acquaintances, those who had causes to petition in the Court, and influential men in various fields of activity. Many excellent pages of Mesonero's *Memorias de un setentón* (*Memoirs of a Septuagenarian*) describe the animated *tertulias* (evening social gatherings) in which colorful and opinionated men allowed their wits to roam spontaneously—at times even in extemporaneous verse.[1] The young Ramón was certainly influenced by his parents' values, but he demonstrates an early independent viewpoint, a trait which will characterize him throughout his life. As a maturing child, he was politically more liberal than his father, although this was somewhat the fashion among the youth. His *Memoirs* demonstrate his early fondness for detached observation and documentation: "All this and many other things I listened to, spurred on by my inborn curiosity and spirit of observation and study" (V, p. 89). The reader perceives a child who smiles amusedly at the events in his home, who injects a certain "distance" but not a tone of superiority between himself and his surroundings. Even as a small child Mesonero was a conscious witness of the times; his *Memoirs* contain anecdotes, popular songs, poems, and factual information including numerous names and dates. While some of this data may come from his memory (a subject to be treated later) and from his family's papers, it seems natural to conclude that he also kept records of his experiences from an early date. As a nine year old, he saved a piece of the infamous low quality bread which fed the poor during the 1811–1812 famine. Later in the century he gave this souvenir to a young friend, the famous novelist Pérez Galdós.

Don Ramón's first years are closely tied, at least in an emotional sense, to the political and social upheaval in Spain after 1807. Much of his later distaste for the external trappings of public politics and his preference for a quiet, stable life may be due to a negative reaction to the tumultuous events of his childhood.

He repeatedly asserts in his *Memoirs* how strongly he was impressed by the flow of tragedy and violence associated with the fall of Carlos IV in March of 1808, the Napoleonic invasion and occupation, and the six year War of Independence. Mesonero's young, impressionable years are filled with instability and, at times, even great tragedy and terror.

During this period he witnessed in Madrid a French military government, a "legal" civilian regime headed by Joseph Bonaparte which had to flee and then return on several occasions, an English military occupation, and even a period in which no governing body was present—not even a Spanish one. Bullets ripped into his house, and he was forced to endure family separation and a period of hiding with friends as well as a constant assault of fears, rumors, and half-truths.

One of the most stark realities any boy could witness befell Ramón during the 1811–1812 famine in Madrid. This bitter hunger, the cause of which is directly related to events of the war, is described in the *Memoirs*:

In truth, the situation of the people of Madrid at that time is unforgettable. Men, women, and children of all description abandoning their miserable dwelling places and dragging themselves in a moribund condition through the streets to beg alms, to snatch even a vegetable stem—something that normally would be placed in the garbage . . . : this display of desperation and anguish; the sight of an infinite number of human beings dying on the streets in broad daylight; the wailing of women and children as they stood beside the corpses of their fathers and brothers, the latter stretched out on the sidewalks and picked up twice daily by the public carts; that prolonged, pitiful groaning of so many unfortunate people gave rise to a gripping terror in the few equally hungry passers-by, and caused the former's faces to take on a cadaverous appearance. The air itself, saturated with the stench of death, seemed to extend a funereal veil over the city, the memory of which causes my mind to freeze over and my pen to become enervated in my hand. Suffice it to say, just for the sake of example, that in the short space of the three hundred steps that separated my house from the primary school, I counted seven dead or dying people one day; I returned to my home crying, and threw myself into the arms of my suffering mother who, in turn, did not allow me to return to school for several months. (V, p. 38.)

In a later paragraph, Mesonero reports that more than twenty thousand inhabitants died of hunger during these months.

Although events in succeeding years may not have proved so dramatic as those of the period 1808–1814, we do know that Spanish history throughout the nineteenth century is marked by deep ideological divisions between liberals and conservatives. These divergencies, extant on the intellectual plane during the previous century, were translated into physical violence in the life span of Mesonero. Periods of tyranny (1814–1820 and 1823–1833) were followed by ultraliberal and moderate periods. Strong censorship, forced exile, loss of position and belongings, and even imprisonment or death befell both liberals such as those who were to become prominent in the Romantic era after 1833 and those *afrancesados* who had demonstrated sympathy with French ideals during the War of Independence. Liberals, progressives, and moderates were often as intolerant and as cruel as their right wing compatriots. New governments, ministries, and constitutions followed each other almost incessantly. Two major civil wars were endured by the people, and there existed many tensions between the northern provinces and centrally located Madrid. Without detailing all of these events— accounts of which are readily available from many sources—it is easy to imagine how a youth might become cynical, even fearful, and acquire a distaste for the struggles and rhetoric of politics. Mesonero preferred a relative anonymity and solid achievement, albeit on a modest scale, to empty promises and constant quarrelling.

II *Schooling and Literary Beginnings*

Little is known about Mesonero's formal education. He provides only sparse reference to the specifics of his private life in his writings. While lacking documentation except for his earliest schooling, we may conclude that Don Ramón never experienced anything beyond the equivalent of high school studies. In 1809 he began primary school under the tutelage of a strict disciplinarian named Tomás Antonio del Campo. After several years and with certain interruptions, one of which has been noted, Don Ramón passed on to other private institutions in which he studied Latin and philosophy. In 1816 a document was issued by his instructor which testifies to the perspicacity, achievement, and good conduct of Mesonero.[2] Later, according to Sainz de Robles and Cotarelo,[3] he pursued his education in the Jesuit school of San Isidro. This latter fact, which goes unmentioned in the *Memoirs*, is somewhat doubted by Seco Serrano.[4] Cotarelo alludes to the most significant aspect of Don Ramón's education:

And with a body of diversified practical knowledge—legal, administrative, ecclesiastical, political, and economic—which he acquired in
his father's office and which he always strove to augment with his
great love for reading (his personal library is the foundation of the
present Municipal Library), Don Ramón was able to enter into
life's struggles in a stronger position than if he had studied at Alcalá
or Salamanca.[5]

Seco Serrano suggests that an 1818 trip to Salamanca might have served to examine the possibility of enrolling at the university; this is unmentioned in Mesonero's accounts of the trip, but we do know that he travelled with a group of students and that in his *Memoirs* he discusses the condition of the university. Don Ramón found the faculty in turmoil due to King Ferdinand's persecution of the liberals. It is possible that he did not enroll because his father was actively engaged in defending the rights of some expelled faculty members.

On January 5, 1820, Don Ramón's father died of apoplexy, thus effectively terminating any plans for the boy's higher education. By 1820 only he, a younger sister, and their mother survived of the original family of seven. Even though only sixteen years old, Ramón had to assume the leadership of his father's successful and demanding business. After a few years the family divested itself of the firm, living off its proceeds plus the rent they collected as property owners. In this fashion, except for the occasional nagging problems of a landlord, Mesonero was free to devote himself entirely to his literary and journalistic pursuits.

Don Ramón's enthusiasm for literature seems to originate in a fortuitous circumstance of 1813. One of the renters responsi-
ble to Don Matías Mesonero was the orchestra director of both

the Cruz and the Príncipe theaters. Instead of paying rent, he
frequently gave the family free passes to the theater. Don
Ramón recalls vividly the enthusiasm with which he attended
many shows, and especially his admiration for the great actor
of the times: Isidoro Máiquez. Mesonero's passion for the stage
never declined. Even though his success in writing original
works or adapting those of others was marginal, he always
attended the theater, commented in his writings upon contemporary and past playwrights, and contributed as an editor to five
volumes on theater in the series *Biblioteca de Autores Españoles.*

We know that Mesonero was an early and avid literary scholar.
In 1816, in the previously mentioned affadavit from his school,
it is mentioned that he "... has succeeded in faithfully translating from the Latin writers, including orators, historians, and
poets."[6] Later, in his *Memoirs,* he mentions that in 1818, while
in Salamanca, he was consumed by memories of the great poetic
tradition of that city. In detailing his thoughts on Luis de León,
Francisco Sánchez, Diego González, Juan Pablo Forner, Meléndez
Valdés, Jovellanos, and others, he reveals that even as a teenager he possessed a solid knowledge of their achievement. He
mentions that his favorite poet was Meléndez Valdés.

Throughout the *Memoirs* Mesonero alludes to his readings
and to his literary predilections. Even previous to his twentieth
birthday, he reveals his passion for the classical Spanish authors
such as Cervantes, Lope de Vega, Calderón de la Barca, Tirso
de Molina, and many more. That he pursued these studies with
vigor is demonstrated by his references to them throughout his
many works as well as by his critical studies and editions of
their works. In 1815, while only twelve years of age, Mesonero
compares his observations of the restored monarchy of Ferdinand VII to his readings. Revealed in the following words is
his early interest in critical, unflattering observation and also
his literary knowledge—the latter mostly obtained in private
study:

All this and many other things I listened to, spurred on by my
inborn curiosity and spirit of observation and study. By chance this
took place at the same time that I found myself caught up, fascinated,
with the reading of *Gil Blas de Santillana,* a book that, with *Don*

Quijote, has always been the object of my enthusiasm. I learned many details about stately gallantry; the actresses and ladies of the Court; the palace intrigues, corrupting ministers, and corrupted favorites; the venality of Court positions and other favors; the bribing of officials; the hypocritical and servile flatterers among the junior officials; and the immorality, in short, the disorder of the social machine. "Well sir," I exclaimed, "all this is the *Court of the Buen Retiro,* reproduced exactly even two centuries later.... All this ... demands a Cervantine pen, and this pen ... will be mine." (V, p. 89)

We know that along with the classics of Latin and Spanish literature, Mesonero was also reading many of the poor quality Spanish translations of foreign (especially French) works that were inundating Spain in the period of Ferdinand VII. With strict censorship and persecution of those who would do more than applaud contemporary realities or write inoffensive escapist drama, there was little to read except foreign translations and originals. Exceptions to this rule are Leandro Fernández de Moratín, José Gallardo, and Sebastián Miñano, all of whom Mesonero cites as contemporary favorites. It is likely that about 1820 Mesonero began to read Jouy, Mercier, and others who may be considered his antecessors in modern *costumbrista* style.

III *On the Threshold*

The date of Mesonero's first creative effort in literature is impossible to fix, but his first "period" covers the span 1820–1823. This is the second constitutional era, a period of relaxed censorship and new freedom of thought and movement. In 1823 Ferdinand would again reinstate his control of thought following the invasion of Spain by the powers of the Holy Alliance.

Don Ramón began by composing poetry and short prose sketches of customs and local characters. The latter form, called *costumbrismo* in Spain, was to become his characteristic vehicle of expression, the form upon which his literary reputation rests. As a poet Mesonero attempted almost every form, especially those characteristic of Neoclassicism, but he recognized his own shortcomings and continued in this genre only sporadically throughout his life. His verse will be briefly studied in a later chapter.

In 1821 a series of prose sketches began to circulate in Madrid. The arrival of many dignitaries in this new constitutional period made Madrid a fertile field for observation and commentary. Cotarelo cites several works as antecedents for Mesonero, including *Condiciones y semblanzas de los Diputados a Cortes para la legislatura de 1820 y 1821* (*Conditions and Likenesses of the Deputies to Congress for the Legislature of 1820 and 1821*), published anonymously but known to be by González Azaola, and Manuel Gorostiza's *Galería de los periodistas, folletinistas y articulistas de Madrid* (*Gallery of Newspapermen, Pamphleteers and Article Writers of Madrid*).[7] The former work is also mentioned by Mesonero as an influence upon his literary beginnings.

At only eighteen years of age, then, Don Ramón composed his first work in prose, sketches of his friends at the Belluzzi dance academy. These portraits went unpublished, and there is no extant manuscript. According to its author, this work circulated privately among friends and their families to everyone's great amusement. A humorous, ironic viewpoint is the central aspect of these sketches.

Much more significant is the next work—also undertaken in 1821—which was published (1822) with noteworthy commercial success. It was entitled *Mis ratos perdidos o ligero bosquejo de Madrid en 1820 y 1821* (*My Free Time or a Quick Outline of Madrid in 1820 and 1821*). Although it has relatively little intrinsic value, this work does, however, loom large in questions dealing with the history of *costumbrismo*. Since this text has been largely unknown until recent years, its discovery has stimulated new discussion. Mesonero himself renounces it as a juvenile effort, even refusing to give its title in his *Memoirs*.

The sketches in *My Free Time* had significant repercussions for our young author. After reading and enjoying these articles, José María de Carnerero, an important editor, invited Mesonero to collaborate with him on the only literary publication in Madrid at the time: *El Indicador de las Novedades, de los Espectáculos y de las Artes*. This marked the beginning of continuing associations by Mesonero with many newspapers and magazines, the vehicle in which he originally published most of his writings. The collaboration with *El Indicador* continued

until early 1823 when the paper became *El Patriota Español,*
evolving into a political tool for the most exalted wing of the
liberal faction. As Mesonero would continue to do throughout
his life, he immediately disassociated himself from these manifestations of extremism.

Throughout 1822, then, Mesonero published short articles
similar to those he had composed in *My Free Time,* epigram-
matic and satirical poetry, and theatrical reviews. Four of these
articles appear in the second volume of *Trabajos no coleccionados*
(*Uncollected Works*), and establish the fact that Mesonero, in
1822, was engaged in publishing articles of *costumbrismo* in the
daily press. They were short, at times quite superficial, but
based upon critical observation of contemporary realities.
Cotarelo, one of the few who has taken these articles into
account, agrees that they fall into the *costumbrista* mold.[8]

The political problems of Spain in 1823—the invasion by the
armies of the Holy Alliance and the subsequent restoration of
Ferdinand VII and his absolute monarchy—touched Mesonero
Romanos personally. Congress, at the beginning of this turbulent
year, decreed a general conscription: each male older than
seventeen was required to serve in the National Militia. Knowing
that the law was coming, Don Ramón "volunteered" in December
of 1822 for this army of the liberal constitutional government.
For several months he performed miscellaneous guard duties
around Madrid. In March he was with the regiment that accompanied King Ferdinand to Cádiz as the Spanish government
fled the invading French army. Mesonero never became involved
in any serious military encounters; in fact, many portions of his
amusing accounts in the *Memoirs* remind the reader of a
picaresque novel. Surprising is the absolute ineffectuality and
informality of this military organization (Mesonero spent several
months apart from his regiment with a friend in Cádiz while
Ferdinand was in Seville). Later in the year, Mesonero travelled
through southern Spain, an experience which became part of
several poems and later some newspaper articles. He finally
returned to Madrid on November 9 after many humorous
escapades.

The government reimposed a strict censorship in 1823; it was
somewhat relaxed after 1825. During the years of most rigid

control, Mesonero Romanos desisted from creative or journalistic writing. Instead he devoted himself to study and to terminating his relationship with his father's business. Until 1830 Don Ramón gave himself to the theater and to collecting materials to be used in his *Manual de Madrid* (*Manual of Madrid*), 1831—a descriptive history of his beloved native city.

Ardent reading, especially of Spain's seventeenth-century theater, soon convinced Don Ramón that many unknown but worthy plays could be enjoyed by a contemporary audience if only someone would correct their formal flaws. Mesonero's deep love for the Baroque theater was always braked by a somewhat paradoxical recognition of its many excesses. His criticism arose from his esthetic principles which were similar to those embraced by Leandro Fernández de Moratín. Moratín, a dramatist always admired and studied by Mesonero, stood for a fairly strict Neoclassic esthetic viewpoint. Mesonero also interpreted Neoclassicism quite rigidly; his usual mode of signalling a poor play was to term it *desarreglado* ("badly arranged"). The question of impact upon public morality was also fundamental for him.

In any case, Mesonero soon accumulated a large personal library of seventeenth-century works, and in 1826 staged his first adaptation, Tirso de Molina's *Amar por señas* (*To Love by Signs*). In the next few years Mesonero succeeded in staging, at times with significant commercial success, other *rifacimenti*. In all they totalled five. His only original full length play, *La señora de protección y escuela de pretendientes* (*The Influence Peddler and Her School for Position Seekers*) was prohibited by the censors. This play was later converted into a prose sketch called *Pretender por alto* (*To Start at the Top*), an article considered one of its author's best.

Don Ramón's final dramatic effort was a translation from the French of a play by Mazères entitled *Marido joven y mujer vieja* (*A Young Husband and an Old Wife*). This work was staged at the Príncipe in 1828. Several critical articles on a new edition of Golden Age plays and on problems of dramatic adaptations were printed in 1828 and 1829 in *El Correo Literario y Mercantil*. The latter was a new periodical of Carnerero's, with whom Mesonero again became associated in the late 1820s.

Don Ramón never tired of studying and commenting upon the contemporary and historical theater; although he would neither write nor adapt more plays after 1828, his dramatic scholarship continued until his death.

During these final years of the 1820s, Mesonero Romanos began an active participation in several informal literary and social groups, making important friends and helping to establish precedents which were, in the next decade, to blossom into several of the most significant learned societies in modern Spanish history.

The first coterie began in 1827 at the home of José Gómez de la Cortina, son of a Spanish count. Among the small group were several youths soon to become famous writers or politicians such as Fermín Caballero, Bretón de los Herreros, Gil y Zárate, Patricio de la Escosura, Ventura de la Vega, and even Mariano José de Larra. Mesonero recalls with satisfaction the laughter provoked as these youths ridiculed the political and literary absurdities of their day. The more serious side of their activity involved collective projects in various municipal and private libraries. Mesonero's interests at this time were principally two: Baroque literature and the history of Madrid, including its buildings, institutions, and traditions.

A second society, mostly social and with some of the same members, was also soon born. Mesonero describes his contributions, referring especially to his own "prodigious memory" and to his "mocking, corrupting wit" (V, p. 161). A significant event occurred in 1830 when several of the outspoken members were arrested by the central government. Mesonero and his mother hurriedly destroyed all the incriminating papers of the young satirist. After the tension passed, the future *costumbrista* pledged again to avoid direct participation in political turmoil, and to rededicate himself to more "directly useful" projects. His anger, though, at this arbitrary repression is not hidden in his *Memoirs*. He refers to the "exalted ignorance," the "suspicious and ignorant censorship," and the "hateful and stupid police," among many other similar comments (V, pp. 157, 162).

This new enthusiasm for literary coteries was to prove irrepressible. With so much opposition to their contemporary political situation as well as their strong interest in Romanticism, these young artists had much to unify them and also to separate them from "official" society. Choosing a dark, tiny café called the Príncipe, they began a regular series of evening meetings which was to prove of immense influence upon literary and other intellectual currents of the next decade. Known as *El Parnasillo*, this group was composed of many of the previously named men plus others such as Espronceda, Estébanez Calderón, Hartzenbusch, and García Gutiérrez. Its single most important contribution was in the dissemination of new ideas; it also became a "literary jury" which passed judgment upon the works and performance of its members. Mesonero boldly states:

From there, from that modest little room came the renovation or the renaissance of our modern theater; from there arose the extremely important *Ateneo científico*; from there the brilliant *Liceo artístico, the Instituto*, and various other literary groups; from there the renovation of schools, of university teaching, and of the press; from there the parliamentary orators and the fiery political speakers that stimulated a complete social transformation. (V, p. 176)

A few years later Mesonero was a major force in the organization and continuation of the *Ateneo* and the *Liceo*. He occupied high positions in both for years.

IV *The Chronicler and the Reformer*

Beginning about 1827, Mesonero Romanos undertook serious study in libraries and private archives, motivated by the desire to prepare a descriptive guidebook of Madrid, one which would prove useful to foreigners and nonnative Madrilenians alike. Of course the voluminous reading and the many interviews and observations also aided him in acquiring knowledge of a more picturesque and moral nature. This information he would later exploit in his *costumbrista* writings. While he prepared, no other up-to-date book of this nature existed, although there were many partial descriptions belonging to previous decades. The most modern of these was the anonymous *Paseo por Madrid o Guía del forastero en la corte* (*Stroll Through Madrid or Guidebook for the Foreigner in Madrid*) of 1815.

Mesonero completed his *Manual de Madrid* in 1830. Publication, however, was delayed until late 1831 due to difficulties with the censor. The *Manual* consists of fourteen chapters, and details the city's history, the biographies of famous sons, and then concentrates on describing Madrid's climate, topography, hotels, government, monuments, and so forth.

The *Manual* was an immediate success. The entire edition was sold in several weeks. After receiving praise from the highest quarters—including the royal family—Mesonero was able to enjoy his first experience in influencing others through literature. His book was extracted in the prestigious *Diccionario geográfico universal* (*Universal Geographic Dictionary*), and a host of manuals and guidebooks appeared in various Spanish capitals. Taking issue with Don Ramón on several points, others began to disseminate pamphlets against certain of his views.

A second edition, with slight changes and additions, appeared in 1833. Then, in 1835, after returning from several years in Europe, Mesonero added an appendix which proposed reforms and improvements based upon his observations in France and England. This *Apéndice al "Manual de Madrid"* is significant because it is the first indication of his depth of feeling and breadth of knowledge concerning urban reform. This interest was to continue, and, to a great extent, become the central focus of Mesonero's life. It should be noted that numerous *costumbrista* articles also contain allusions or entire sections dealing with Madrid's history or needed material improvements. In cooperation with certain civic officials, many of these proposals were realized quickly; others were to preoccupy Mesonero for years.

In 1844 a larger, more systematic, and better written *Manual* was composed. This may be considered the third version, and carried a modified title and a new interior organization.

In 1846 Mesonero broke with one of his self-imposed rules, and accepted election to the Madrid City Council. Later, however, he would refuse all other positions that could be considered political, including mayor of the city. He served in the council four years, and his work bore many practical fruits. Also, in 1846, he presented a new work called *Proyecto de mejoras generales de Madrid* (*Plan for General Improvements in Madrid*). Many rather revolutionary notions were proposed, including a limited expansion of the city. Most of his ideas were translated into reality at one time or another.

Various other minor works dealing with civic betterment were published in these years. For example, Mesonero rewrote the Municipal Ordinances in 1847. The council quickly approved and published his version.

In 1854 Mesonero published a fourth and greatly expanded *Manual*. Then, in 1861, he concluded *El antiguo Madrid (Ancient Madrid)*, a long, interesting re-creation of the history of his loved city from the earliest times to the present. This work was published first as articles in *El Semanario Pintoresco Español*.

It would take a separate book—and works of this nature do exist—to detail Mesonero's positive accomplishments in Madrid's civic affairs. He is known for his intervention in cultural, economic, educational, social, and architectural matters. He was the motivating force behind the reestablishment of the *Ateneo* (1835), a savings bank for the poor, a modern asylum for the indigent, and innumerable new streets, plazas, and buildings. One of his passions was the preservation of important historical sites such as the birthplaces of Madrid's famous sons. Mesonero also served as an official in many of these new organizations while they were laying their foundations.

V *Mesonero's Travels Abroad*

Reference has already been made to a trip to France and England in 1833 and 1834. Discounting his travels within Spain such as the 1823 trek to the South as a militia recruit, Don Ramón made three major trips in his lifetime. The first two were of special significance because they allowed him to make observations—both of a material and moral nature—which he would continue to call upon in his writings and public life.

After arriving in France in late 1833, Don Ramón was informed of the death of Spain's monarch. Resisting the temptation to return, he continued through France and also visited England where he viewed the first railroads. After ten months he returned to Madrid in May of 1834.

We have already mentioned the proposed urban reforms contained in the 1835 appendix to the *Manual of Madrid* which were a direct result of this trip. This trip stimulated the commencement of Mesonero's civic activism. Scattered newspaper articles of a reformist nature were also published upon his return in the *Diario de Madrid,* a newspaper over which he assumed direction in 1835 in order to have a wider forum for his reform-oriented thought.

A second trip in 1840 and 1841 to France and Belgium resulted in a book entitled *Recuerdos de viaje por Francia y Bélgica en 1840 y 1841 (Memoirs of a Journey Through France and Belgium in 1840 and 1841).* This trip was specifically made to complete the author's knowledge regarding modern technological advancements in these two industrializing nations. Curious are the highly detailed accounts of even seemingly trite matters such as the condition of sidewalks and the lack of unsupervised children and dogs in the streets. A balance is maintained between that which he considers superior and also inferior to the realities of his native country.

While returning to Spain, Don Ramón stopped in Paris to witness the transfer of the Emperor Napoleon's remains. The winter cold was so intense that he lost the greatest part of his sense of hearing. This defect was to materially affect his life; for example, he was unable to participate actively in meetings such as those of the Royal Spanish Academy due to his deafness.

A final trip to France was undertaken in 1865, but has no significant bearing upon subsequent thought or writings.

VI *Mesonero, the Costumbrista*

On January 12, 1832, Mesonero Romanos published an article in *Cartas Españolas* which was to become known as his first sketch of manners. While this assertion may be disputed, we do know that *El retrato (The Picture)* marks the beginning of a new phase of continuous writings, and that its quality far surpasses any previous efforts. These articles concentrate upon the moral rather than the physical Madrid; in them Mesonero expressly attempts the difficult task of verbally capturing a society undergoing rapid transformation. Contrasts between old and new ways are one of the basic means by which he alludes to societal divisions, contradictions, and change. Some are bitterly ironic, others are much more festive and inoffensive, but together these short sketches offer glimpses of every social class as well as many public places and dark corners of the city.

The Picture was signed by *Un curioso parlante* (*A Curious Chatterbox*), the beginning of a long association by Mesonero with this pseudonym.

Later in 1832 the *Cartas Españolas* became known as the *Revista Española,* and Mesonero continued using it to publish articles dealing with customs and civic realities. The principal development in these years was his founding of *El Semanario Pintoresco Español* on April 3, 1836. Since the death of King Ferdinand in 1833, a new freedom of expression existed in Spain; in spite of this liberty, few exclusively literary or artistic magazines succeeded. For example, the *Revista Española* had a definite political purpose. In 1835 *El Artista,* a review devoted to the poetry of Romanticism, commenced and promptly failed. Mesonero's good fortune with *El Semanario Pintoresco Español,* then, was a significant occurrence in Spanish journalism. Don Ramón personally controlled his magazine until 1842 when he sold it. It continued with less success until 1857, an extraordinary story for the times.

Mesonero aspired to reach a wider audience in *El Semanario Pintoresco Español* by treating diverse topics, most of them dealing with Spanish art, monuments, biography, and regional customs. He also carefully avoided political controversy. At one point under his editorship the circulation reached 5,000 subscribers. Counted among the collaborators were such men as Roca de Togores, Eugenio Ochoa, Gil y Zárate, José Zorrilla, Clemente Díaz, Juan Hartzenbusch, and Enrique Gil. Mesonero's format was copied from his observations of the *Penny Magazine* in London and *Le Magasin Pittoresque* of Paris. A definite contribution was made by his importation and popularization of the wood engraving. He brought foreign experts in the field to teach his own workmen, and also sent the latter abroad to improve their technique. The illustrated magazine in Spain owes a debt to Mesonero Romanos.

The decade of the 1830s represents the apogee of Mesonero's "moral" *costumbrismo* just as the following ten year span marks the height of his civic writings and activities. After publishing the majority of his articles in *El Semanario Pintoresco Español,* he began, in 1835, to gather them in book form. The first group of three volumes is known as the *Panorama matritense* (*Pano-*

rama of Madrid); later, in 1842, he published all of his previous writings in this vein, now calling the totality *Escenas matritenses* (*Scenes of Madrid*). This work is the most important basis of Don Ramón's literary reputation. Several of the articles have become classical anthology pieces. Its success was noteworthy; by 1851 the *Scenes of Madrid* had passed through five editions; their appearance in the periodical press is counted as the first.

The final major contribution of Mesonero to *costumbrismo* was made in 1862 when a new volume entitled *Tipos, grupos y bocetos de cuadros de costumbres* (*Types, Groups and Outlines of Costumbrista Sketches*) was published. This work was one volume in a new four volume collection of his writings called *Obras jocosas y satíricas del Curioso Parlante* (*Jocose and Satiric Works of the Curious Chatterbox*). This latter multiple volume work also went through new editions in the nineteenth century.

VII *The Final Years*

Mesonero continued to live at his birthplace on Olivo Street until 1836 when he moved to a street today called Aduana. His last residence was in a home he constructed in 1846 at Bilbao Square. This house was built on the lot of a former convent after Mesonero acquired the property at a government auction.

Don Ramón's personal life entered a new phase in 1849 when the long time bachelor married Salomé de Ichaso. Even though only twenty-two, she lived happily with the aging author until the latter's death. Four children outlived their father.

Continuing to write until just days before his death, Don Ramón spent his last decades devoted to his home, his studies, and the duties related to several positions of prestige which he held. He published numerous newspaper articles in these years, but few could be termed *costumbrista*. Most treated literary history, biography, and Madrid's past. Mesonero had been named chronicler of Madrid in 1864, and he took the duties seriously. Other articles of this period deal principally with the writer's contemporary circumstances; he describes new editions of interest, notable dramatic performances, and important anniversaries. Many of these articles can be found in two posthumous works his sons dedicated to his memory: *Algo en prosa y en verso inédito* (*Some Unpublished Prose and Verse*), 1883, and *Trabajos no coleccionados* (*Uncollected Works*) in two volumes of 1903 and 1905. Also in this vein are the prologues and catalogues he contributed to five volumes in the *Biblioteca de Autores Españoles* series. These studies represent amplification of previously published brief articles; they were completed during the final years of the 1850s.

Mention has been made of Mesonero's large personal library. It was composed principally of choice volumes on the history of Madrid and on Spanish drama. In 1875 he published a fifty-six page catalogue of his holdings.[9] In 1876 the City Council purchased a major portion of Mesonero's library in order to commence a long-postponed Municipal Library. Don Ramón was named director of the library; in 1877 he published the first index of its possessions.[10]

Mesonero's final significant literary endeavor was the publication in 1880—first as newspaper articles—of his *Memoirs of a Septuagenarian*. It is to these that we have referred for many biographical facts. An enjoyable interweaving of public history, private experiences, and general anecdotes, this volume captures the flavor of early nineteenth-century history. Such renowned writers as Benito Pérez Galdós availed themselves generously of its contents for documentation of their own literary output. This popular work has passed through many reprintings, the last one occurring in 1961.

On April 29, 1882, Mesonero suffered a stroke which caused his death the following day. He was buried in the San Isidro Cemetery with—it is said—ten thousand persons in attendance. His wife survived him for twelve years.

VIII A Citizen Recognized

One major theme in Don Ramón's life and writings is his passion for independence. Not only did he seek and attain financial security, he also sought freedom from political, social, literary, and all other compromises. Throughout his life he alludes to this feeling in his literary texts. At one point he composed a long poem on this subject which he published as an adjunct to the *Memoirs*. We have seen how he finally accepted a four year post with the City Council only after being urged by others for eleven years, and because he felt he could serve the city most effectively in that manner. He rejected countless other similar opportunities, even the position of mayor of Madrid. It was Mesonero's opinion that his calling was that of a critical observer; if he were in allegiance to a political party or social philosophy, he would not have the necessary flexibility as a commentator.

Nevertheless, throughout his life Mesonero did serve publicly, especially for brief spans on a voluntary basis in the directorship of socially oriented organizations which he helped create. To single out only a few, he was director of the Savings Association from 1853–1855, president of the Urban Sanitation Board in 1858, and secretary of the Fire Insurance Society in 1836. Don Ramón was also vice-president and librarian (elected three times) of the *Ateneo,* librarian of the *Liceo,* and official and senior chronicler of Madrid from 1864 on. Politically, besides the City Council, Mesonero served as a provincial deputy in 1858, and, in 1881, was named honorary lifetime director of the Property Owners Association. In the same year he was named lifetime director of the Municipal Library and chief of its archives. Although he fled honors and public recognition, he did receive the Cross of Carlos III in 1838 in the company of Agustín Durán, and in 1871, the Great Cross of Isabel the Catholic. A complete list of his many public activities and honors can be found in the appendix of volume two of *Uncollected Works.*

Only two honors ever caught Mesonero's imagination. He was especially proud of being Madrid's chronicler, and also of his call to the Royal Spanish Academy in 1838. He was an honorary member of the Academy until 1847 when he was given regular status. His academy discourse deals with the history of the novel in Spain; it was pronounced on May 17, 1838.

Because of his deafness, Mesonero was not always able to participate actively in the Academy's sessions. He did, however, make long-remembered contributions. For example, in 1861, it was Don Ramón who discovered the house in which Lope de Vega died, and who proposed a monument worthy of the Golden Age playwright. On November 25, 1862, three hundred years after his birth, Lope was accorded an elaborate ceremony including a worthy sculptured monument—all this in the presence of the city's highest dignitaries. Years later, during the frenzy of the September Revolution of 1868, a sister in the Trinitarian Convent advised Mesonero that plans were being readied for the destruction of their edifice. Since the remains of Miguel de Cervantes were located there, it was felt that there existed even more reason to halt this destructive act. Mesonero intervened, received a pledge from the government that the convent would be respected, and was instrumental in placing several inscriptions there to advise future generations of the grave of Cervantes. It seems poetic justice that Mesonero Romanos should in some way contribute to the memory of the author of *Don Quijote*; the latter had been the single most influential force in molding Don Ramón's literary style.

Mesonero was remembered posthumously by several impressive ceremonies and monuments. In 1883, Olivo Street was renamed after the author of *Scenes of Madrid*, and, two years later, a commemorative inscription was placed by the City Council at his Bilbao Street residence. In 1887 the Madrilenian Economic Society published the proceedings of a special gathering held in his honor, and, finally, in 1903—one hundred years after his birth—a bust was unveiled on the Paseo de Recoletos; today this monument is located in the Pedro Ribera Gardens. A re-creation of Mesonero's home office can be found in the Hemeroteca Municipal of Madrid.

IX *The Man in Retrospect*

Certain character traits can be extracted from the foregoing description of Mesonero Romanos. Apart from his fierce desire for independence, the principal passion in Don Ramón's life was Madrid. The rush to honor Mesonero during his final years and following his death gives eloquent testimony to his recognized contributions. Although his *costumbrista* writings and his social activities seem separate on the surface, in truth they were closely intertwined. All of them deal with some aspect of Madrid. Even his travel memoirs make constant reference by comparison to his native city.

Too much can be made of Mesonero's bourgeois origins and life style. With the discredit into which the middle class has fallen today, some writers allude to this aspect in a denigrating manner. Mesonero was, in fact, devoted to the least fortunate of society. Some of his works have been described above. Central to his philosophy and to the institutions which he helped establish was an awareness that charity goes beyond the material. Reeducation, self-help, work, and psychological aid always form a part of his thought. It is true that Mesonero was utilitarian. He lacked a university education, but nevertheless was able to carve a niche for himself quite apart from his family's commercial orientation. Some of his statements regarding elementary education foreshadow later liberal attitudes in Spain; he sought an open, free atmosphere in which the child or adult would learn by doing.

Several almost contradictory attitudes run through this author's writings. Everyone who reads his works is impressed by the frequent references to himself in the most humble terms. For example, he affirms in his *Memoirs* that the popularity of his *My Free Time* only proves the lamentable state into which Spanish letters had fallen before Romanticism. He seems to recognize throughout his life his role as a humble contributor to a minor genre. He refers to his style as plain, simple, and unadorned. However, on many occasions the intended irony of his claims to humility is not difficult to perceive; it quickly becomes a pose.

Parallel to his proclaimed humility is a certain pride, especially with reference to specific topics. Mesonero was extremely defensive about his position vis-à-vis Mariano José de Larra and Estébanez Calderón. He insists on being considered the first *costumbrista*. Another reiterated claim is for the objectivity and truthfulness of his descriptions. He also insists with less offensive boastfulness that future generations should be grateful to his own contemporaries for vast improvements in the physical aspects of Madrid.

More in line with his modesty is a trait which no one can miss upon reading Mesonero's work. Don Ramón had a passion for preserving the privacy of his personal, intimate life. Even in his *Memoirs* one searches in vain for details about his family or about any aspect of his private world. Personal emotion is only present as it may be directed to external realities. Speculations which some critics have made regarding unfortunate amorous ties in his youth are based on extremely flimsy grounds.

Don Ramón, in his later years, manifests through his letters to such novelists as Pérez Galdós and José María de Pereda that he indeed admired new trends toward Realism in the novel. He also conveys his satisfaction when Galdós, for example, recognizes his contributions to the incipient novel. It seems that Mesonero relished his long conversations with Galdós which allowed the latter to better document his series of *Episodios nacionales* (*National Episodes*).

Don Ramón gives every indication of being practical and unsentimental about his personal finances. For example, he was not above profiting in 1836 from the auction of usurped religious property; also, in 1876, he sold some of his personal library to the municipality for 70,000 *reales*. Seco Serrano suggests convincingly that considering his well-stocked finances, one could have expected more generosity toward the city.

A final outstanding character trait was his curiosity. His pseudonym, "The Curious Chatterbox," seems well chosen. His lengthy walks to every corner of Madrid foreshadow the strolls of Pérez Galdós. These outings continued until two days before his death. The letters of his last years give testimony to his active brain; he beseeched Pereda, Galdós, Alarcón, and others to give him their latest works the moment they were published. Days afterward each writer could count on a return note with some critical reaction. Finally, Mesonero never stopped his civic activity nor his periodical or book-length publication. His last article—on Moratín—was published four days before his death.

Physically Mesonero was rather stout; he used glasses for his nearsightedness, and, according to many observers, normally exhibited a smile that had a quick ironic turn. Pérez Galdós wrote several portraits of Don Ramón; in them he emphasized the above features plus our author's happy, healthy appearance; his simple, undistinguished gestures; a tendency to speak loudly because of his near deafness; and an animated, charming manner of conversation. Galdós also mentions "... that constant habit of clasping his hands behind his back, as though they presented an obstacle to him in his stately investigative travels."[11]

CHAPTER 2

Genre, Sources, and Esthetic Principles

AS an inveterate collector of historical texts, a literary scholar-critic, and a European traveller, Mesonero Romanos experienced numerous opportunities to familiarize himself with past literary trends. Also, he was highly analytical of his own writings, frequently making explicit his opinions regarding the origin of his inspiration, his evolution in style and themes, the purposes which he sought to fulfill, and the esthetic merit of his articles. Lomba y Pedraja refers to Don Ramón as a lifelong "... professional and master in his genre."[1]

After some basic definitions and a brief description of the literary tradition—both domestic and foreign—into which Mesonero fits, we will allude to the problem of his sources, to his literary relations with his contemporaries, and then detail his most representative statements regarding his own art.

I Spanish Antecedents

The principal literary achievements of Don Ramón fit into a mode known as *costumbrismo*. Loosely defined, this minor genre is composed of brief animated descriptions—in prose or verse—of typical scenes, human types, or customs. Written at times in a tone of ironic censure, on other occasions these sketches are intended merely as a diversion or a pastime; in the latter case the tone is festive, sentimental, or objective. Usually a weak plot line provides an underlying framework, although occasionally the principal unity is merely that of the writer's point of view. As Montesinos points out, when the interest shifts away from description to the narrative line or to the psychological dimension of the characters, these *cuadros* ("pictures") can approximate the short story.[2] When, however, the principal element

39

is the overall scene or the representativeness of the characters, then a comparison to the essay is more apt.

Many critics feel that nineteenth-century Spanish *costumbrismo* has a long, continuous native tradition. Margarita Ucelay Da Cal sees this style as part of the national character: "The realism of our literature, its moralistic and satirical tradition, . . . the lack of affinity for abstract thought, the pictorial sense and the enjoyment of the reproduction of immediate reality, these are indications that *costumbrismo* fits in perfectly with the nation's esthetic character."[3]

It will be argued in this study that *costumbrismo* had its origins in the middle and late seventeenth century, but that significant differences between this late Baroque manifestation and those that follow make misleading the indiscriminate use of the term. The internal development necessary to give Spanish *costumbrismo* enough independent features to permit its denotation as a separate genre does not reach its apex until the decade of the 1830s. However, *costumbrista* articles similar to those of the Mesonero period began to appear sporadically in the preceding century and especially after 1817. Some critics, using the word with great latitude, have stated that *costumbrismo* can be found even in the Middle Ages and early Renaissance. Writers who at times give glimpses of daily life, such as Juan Ruiz, Alfonso Martínez de Toledo, Antonio de Torquemada, and Eugenio Salazar, are cited as early *costumbristas*.[4] Along these same lines, others have mentioned many short *pasos* ("skits"), *entremeses* ("interludes"), and isolated scenes from longer plays authored by such men as Lope de Rueda, Quiñones de Benavente, Lope de Vega, and Cervantes. On the other extreme, those who use a narrow definition of *costumbrismo* see its commencement either about 1820 with Sebastián Miñano or others, or a decade later when Estébanez Calderón, Larra, and Mesonero began to publish regularly. Several relatively recent studies exemplify this tendency: Le Gentil mentions 1817 and F. Courtney Tarr points to 1828 as the best date for its beginnings. Further confusion is added when Clifford Montgomery insists upon 1750 as the true commencement.

The resolution of this and other difficulties is complex if not impossible. There is no line which satisfactorily delimits this genre, separating it neatly from the moralistic-ascetic treatise, the urban guidebook, the political satire, the sociological essay or article, the short story, and specific episodes of the picaresque novel. While matters such as ultimate intention and external form may vary within an article of *costumbres,* it seems essential that it be relatively brief, mostly descriptive, and formally autonomous—not predominantly submerged in another genre such as an essay, a novel, or a play. When the latter occurs, it seems preferable to speak of *costumbrista* elements.

Unmistakable manifestations of these "elements" do appear in the seventeenth century; Cervantes' *Rinconete y Cortadillo,* Quevedo's *Buscón (The Swindler)* and *Sueños (Visions),* Vélez de Guevara's *El diablo cojuelo (The Lame Devil)* along with many other picaresque novels, and certain writings of Gracián, Castillo Solórzano, and Salas Barbadillo provide good examples. Many of these Golden Age works exploit local color descriptions from time to time, although generally these are small parts of a large whole. A strong presence of moralistic satire and censure also takes away from the independence of the scene itself. Of all the early works, *Rinconete y Cortadillo* most clearly fulfills the requisites of the evolving *costumbrista* genre.

In a more intense and exact fashion, however, a strong *costumbrista* tendency does emerge about the middle of the seventeenth century. Correa Calderón refers to this period as that of the disintegration of the novel into a loosely woven episodical structure with a fusion of the picaresque, courtly, and moralistic-ascetic modes.[5] The results are best demonstrated in the satirical-didactic prose of Antonio Liñán y Verdugo, Juan de Zabaleta, and Francisco Santos. Rather than creators of a new genre, however, these three represent the end of a cycle, the disintegration of the Baroque novel. Their writings differ from those which later appear in the periodical press in that the sketches still possess only a relative autonomy. The novelistic framework, although weakened, is still present. Also, in some cases, these descriptions seem principally to function as examples or case histories for sermonlike moralistic discourses. The confusion of genres is pronounced.

Similar to much imaginative literature in the period, a general decline both in quantity and quality affects the development of *costumbrismo* from approximately 1660 to 1750. The end of the Baroque period, the economic and social decline of Spain, a change in royal dynasties (1700), a thirteen year War of Succession, and a period of instability and adjustments to new institutions are some of the causes for this phenomenon. The only significant manifestation occurs in 1729 when Fulgencio Afán de Ribera publishes his pamphlet *Virtud al uso y mística a la moda* (Stylish Virtue and Fashionable Mysticism). In this work a father instructs his son, a neophyte priest, on the best ways to employ a false religiosity in order to prosper in life. In form and conception, this work resembles those of Liñán and Santos, but its strong censure not only of hypocrisy but of certain religious practices foretells the more secular viewpoint of modern literature. Also modern is its form of publication: the separate pamphlet. In a sense, then, *Stylish Virtue* can be said to connect the past with the future.

The rise of new types of publications and the increased reading audience—a direct benefit of the French Enlightenment —are the strongest conditioning factors in the emergence of modern *costumbrismo*. Keynotes in this form are brevity and an amenable, popular style. Neither of these factors was present in seventeenth-century book length publications. The new period, furthermore, witnesses the arrival of the literary or semiliterary newspaper, the magazine, and the tract or pamphlet. Obviously, the pressures of space, the frequency of publication, and the need to be concerned with commercial success brought about the "purer" *costumbrista* sketches. Now divorced from the novel or treatise, the article could be devoted simply to one representative type or scene. The first literary periodical was the *Diario de los literatos* of 1737. Montgomery finds the first use of the word *cuadro* in 1787 in *El correo de los ciegos de Madrid*; he infers from this a growing awareness of the formal traits of the genre.

New forms allied to the newspaper and developed in the eighteenth century soon emerged. Typically, the essays associated with *costumbrismo* were published as separate pamphlets or as articles, editorials, or letters to the editor. Often the editor would sign ficticious names to letters he himself penned. Soon pseudonyms such as Clavijo y Fajardo's *El Pensador* ("The

Thinker") were common. The popularity of many of these publications is demonstrated by their repeated republication in bound volumes throughout the century.

Without doubt the newspaper and magazine with their frequently anonymous writers contributed most to this incipient minor genre. Nevertheless, just as in centuries past, there were numerous well-known writers who advanced its mentality and forms in their full length works. In this vein we can cite José Cadalso in his *Cartas marruecas* (*Moroccan Letters*) and *Los eruditos a la violeta* (*Violet-Water Scholars*), Torres Villarroel in his *Vida* (*Life*) and *Sueños morales* (*Moral Visions*), Padre Isla's *Fray Gerundio* (*Brother Gerundio*), and the pamphlets of Juan Pablo Forner. The short theatrical farces called *sainetes* may have been the single most important contributor apart from the press. Ramón de la Cruz and González del Castillo, especially the former, were masters of depicting popular scenes and types in a racy, true-to-life fashion. Correa Calderón aptly equates the farce and the article of customs to the full length play and the novel respectively.[6]

Space limitations prevent a review of the many short-lived periodicals which carried examples of this nascent style. Montgomery opines that the first worthy example is the pamphlet published in 1750 by Eugenio García Baragaña entitled *Noche Phantástica* (*Fantastic Night*). In reality, this is a treatise on the technique of bullfighting; the *costumbrista* content is diffuse and typical of many previous works. Other significant contributors who can be identified by name are Juan Antonio Mercadel, Beatriz Cienfuegos, Juan Antonio Zamácola, Santos Manuel Rubín de Celis y Noriega, Cristóbal Romea y Tapia, and Lucas Alemán. Most of these and other *"costumbristas"* are obscure journalists, many of whom are difficult to identify due to their pseudonyms or their complete anonymity. It seems probable that some articles have been wrongly attributed to a journal's editor for lack of better evidence. Again, much of this writing is polemical and not relatively disinterested scenic description. For example, Romea y Tapia is frequently engaged in ideological warfare with the *afrancesados*.

The most influential of the eighteenth-century precursors is José Clavijo y Fajardo (1726–1806). Educated in France, he edited several important periodicals including *El Mercurio*. Governmental intervention for purposes of theater reform was a basic theme of this journalist. Clavijo was devoted to publicizing the "progressive" French customs; he founded the century's most important journal, *El Pensador* (modelled after Joseph Addison's *The Spectator*), and translated many works from the French. Because of its impact, similar magazines appeared in Spain and in America, all of which employed the word *pensador* ("thinker") in the title.

Clavijo openly expressed his lack of interest in criticism and reformation—just as did Mesonero later—but, in reality, his acrimonious pen was didactically oriented. Montgomery lucidly observes that Clavijo diminishes the personal touch, the specificity of his *cuadros*, as compared to the masters of this genre; this essaylike quality is a product of the didacticism which informs his writings. In spite of this, Montgomery concludes that at least twelve examples of *costumbrismo* can be found in the eighty-six essays of *El Pensador*; he also affirms that Clavijo, in his statement of purpose and in certain articles, has demonstrably influenced both Larra and Mesonero.[8]

The unsettled political conditions after 1808 together with two periods of harsh censure stifle the continuation of critical sketches and open polemics. *Costumbrismo* is a mode which can only flourish in periods of tranquility. Freedom to observe and report openly, without fear of repression, is essential. Also, without stability, very few have either the time or the money to read literature marginal to the conflicts of the times. Even more important, a decree of 1815 prohibited in Spain the publication of all but two official newspapers. About 1818, however, this law was relaxed.

In 1820, with the second constitutional period, a new stage in journalism is begun. Additional newspapers appear—some of them devoted largely to the arts—and the pamphlet becomes principally a tool for political extremism. *Costumbrismo* follows the fate of the newspaper after this date.

We have already observed that in 1822 Mesonero becomes associated with Carnerero's *El Indicador* and publishes *costumbrista* articles. Other important papers which also carry these sketches are *La Minerva o el Revisor General* (1817–1818),

La Crónica Científica y Literaria (1817–1818), and *El Correo Literario y Mercantil* (1828–1833). As mentioned above, certain scholars have singled out articles in these and other papers, calling each of them the first true manifestation of Spanish *costumbrismo*.

When analyzing individual writers of this period, it is clear that Eugenio de Tapia and Sebastián Miñano y Bedoya are the most influential for later developments. M. E. Porter observes that a short pamphlet of 1807 by Tapia called *El viaje de un curioso por Madrid* (*Travels of a Curious Man Through Madrid*) prefigures Mesonero's *My Free Time* and was surely known by the latter.[9] Most influential upon Mesonero, according to Ucelay Da Cal, was a new objectivity of observation and a festive tone.[10] Tapia also published other comparable articles in the press.

Many literary manuals affirm that Sebastián Miñano, especially with his *Lamentos políticos del pobrecito holgazán* (*Political Lamentations of a Poor Idler*) of 1820, creates the modern form of the *costumbrista* essay. Lately, however, after more study, much disagreement has emerged. It is now generally concluded that this publication is principally a political and religious tract. Ucelay Da Cal opines that any *costumbrismo* is only background for Miñano's attacks against absolutism and repression.[11] Miñano has only substituted politics for the moralization of the seventeenth and the ideology of the eighteenth centuries. The liberal-oriented political tone does, nevertheless, parallel the later mood of many of Larra's articles.

II   *Foreign Antecedents*

Without ignoring the weight of national tradition, it must be observed that the immediate stimulus for Mesonero, Larra, and Estébanez Calderón was not national but foreign. From England and France came certain influences which each admitted as decisive. In general terms the original stimulus and the most important models are foreign, but soon a reconciliation between national and foreign currents was accomplished. A third factor in this amalgamation is the individual creativity of each artist: each injected his own personality and the spirit of his times to the above two factors.

To gain perspective on the question of foreign influences, we must turn our gaze again to the Spanish picaresque novel, beginning with *Lazarillo de Tormes* in 1554. As is known, these works were episodical, descriptive, critical, and, after the sixteenth century, incorporated large quantities of moralization. Translated into the principal European languages, these works quickly passed through numerous editions. Detailed studies by F. W. Chandler, W. S. Hendrix, and Ucelay Da Cal have convincingly established the penetration of the Spanish picaresque genre into England and France, and also its molding force upon these countries' prose forms.[12] The two most immediate Spanish influences, for example, upon the original English *costumbristas* were Quevedo with his *Sueños* (*Visions*), 1627, and Vélez de Guevara with his *El diablo cojuelo* (*The Lame Devil*), 1641. These two authors were well known in England about 1700, Quevedo by means of a popular English translation and Vélez de Guevara through an English translation of Lesage's adaptation into French in 1707 called *Le Diable boiteux* (*The Devil upon Two Sticks*). In any case, although the names and a few characteristics are different, Guevara's utilization of the observant devil as a commentator upon manners was incorporated immediately into French and English *costumbrismo*. In the hands of Lesage he becomes known as Asmodée; Steele and Addison baptize him Pacolet.

Of course, Spain was not unique in its cultivation of moralization based on contemporary observation during the seventeenth century. A significant counterpart to Zabaleta, and even a possible influence upon the English, for example, was the Frenchman Jean de La Bruyère (1645–1696). His incisive epigrams, essays, and portraits in *Les Caractères ou les moeurs de ce siècle* (*Characters or the Manners of This Age*) depicted the manners of his age and communicated his opposition to exploitation and injustice. La Bruyère's socially directed criticism seems more modern than that of his contemporary Spaniards. He was well known and admired by Mesonero Romanos.

In 1709 England's Richard Steele established a thrice weekly magazine called *The Tatler*, an extremely significant act in the history of the sketch of manners. His purpose was to offer critically and humorously his impressions of current events and manners. Soon Joseph Addison was writing for *The Tatler*;

when this journal became defunct in 1711, both authors created *The Spectator*. Ucelay Da Cal asserts that *The Spectator* became the model for European middle class periodical literature of the eighteenth century.[13] Clavijo y Fajardo (*El Pensador*) was one who admitted his indebtedness. Addison soon became a byword for French and Spanish commentators. Recently, G. T. Northrup asserted that the "sketch" was born as a separate literary form in *The Spectator*.[14] In England the spirit of this journal was continued by Samuel Johnson in *The Rambler* (1750–1752) and in his "The Idler" essays contributed to the *Universal Chronicle* between 1758 and 1760.

Until the twentieth century, few Spanish writers had direct contact with literature written in English. The reverse of this statement is also true, though probably to a lesser degree. French often served as an intermediary language for literary relations between Spain and England. We have seen how the picaresque novel, especially *The Lame Devil*, entered England through a translation of a French adaptation. In the same way, Clavijo y Fajardo knew Addison only through the French. Even at the time of Mesonero it was only possible to read brief translated passages of Addison. Most knew of him through his commentators and imitators.

By far the most successful imitator for the Spaniards was Victor-Joseph Ètienne, known as de Jouy (or simply Jouy), his place of birth. Spanish writers read Jouy's works in French or in translation, but fully recognized the latter's debt to Addison, a debt the Frenchman himself honorably admitted. All three of the principal Spanish *costumbristas* explicitly alluded to Jouy's importance in their development: Larra was the most outspoken in this regard. Jouy, a minor if not unknown figure in French literature, wrote insignificant plays and was a member of the academy, but was principally a journalist. During the second decade of the nineteenth century, he penned numerous prose sketches of urban and rural scenes which he first published in newspapers such as *La Gazette de France*. Later these articles were collected in bound volumes, at least seven of which were owned by Mesonero.

The earliest works of Mesonero and Larra manifest these writers' acquaintance with Jouy's publications. Nevertheless, even earlier recognition is due the Frenchman. Le Gentil points to an article of 1817 in *La Minerva o el Revisor General,* affirming it was clearly inspired by Jouy. In fact, this periodical's editor, Pedro María de Olive, bows to the Frenchman in the same year: ". . . an ingenious writer and a very fine and sagacious observer who has excelled in a genre that the English perfected."[15] In 1828, another *costumbrista,* Mariano de Rementería y Fica, dedicates his writings to Jouy. In summary, this Frenchman served as a primary stimulus and model during the first decades of the nineteenth century for the new brilliance of descriptive writing in Spain.

Other Frenchmen, some similar to Jouy and others more ideologically or politically oriented, also were known in Spain. References to their inspiration can be found in many of the *costumbristas,* including Mesonero. The most important of these secondary figures was Louis-Sébastien Mercier. Mercier did not use the press and did not write true articles of manners, but Ucelay Da Cal suggests that Mesonero probably owes the basic plan and divisions of *Scenes of Madrid* to this author and his *Le Tableau de Paris* (*Scenes of Paris*). Paul-Louis Courier and Henri Monnier are others mentioned as sources by Spanish *costumbristas.* Jouy himself mentions Abbé Prévost and Pierre Marivaux: the latter published his own periodical, *Le Spectateur Français* (1720–1724), modelled after Joseph Addison's *The Spectator.*

The reciprocity between Spain and England is obvious from the above historical résumé. England received its original inspiration from Spain, principally through the French language. In turn, eighteenth- and nineteenth-century Spanish *costumbristas* received their original stimulation to write and to modernize the genre (especially to diminish the moralization) from the English through French imitators. Because so much of the original input was Spanish, it is easy to understand why men such as Mesonero—well acquainted with their national tradition—were so receptive to the modern proddings. After Jouy's writings became promulgated about 1817, Spanish *costumbrismo* moved toward independence in terms of genre, and culminated in what F. C. Tarr refers to as the most significant prose manifestation during the Romantic epoch.[16]

III   *Mesonero's Principal Sources*

The complete identification of Mesonero's primary and second-ary sources of inspiration poses difficult problems; to judge by the contradictory views of previous critics, the difficulty is unresolvable without a new focus. Many of these statements are based upon an original prejudice for or against Mesonero, or for or against Spain and its literature. Extremes are reached: some have argued that Don Ramón created the *cuadro de costum-bres*,[17] others insist he normally wrote by servile imitation—especially of Jouy.[18]

In effect, there are difficulties. A principal problem is that Mesonero frequently comments upon his literary debts, but not always with total consistency. In general, Mesonero tends to explicitly recognize his sources, especially the foreign ones, during the first years of his literary career. As an older man, he gives more emphasis to his own originality and to the Spanish *costumbrista* tradition. It has been suggested that his early recognition of Jouy, Mercier, and Addison was partially an attempt to give added prestige to his writings and to his genre.[19]

Another difficulty is the great body of descriptive literature extant in most Western European countries since the seventeenth century. Since Mesonero knew several foreign literatures well, especially French, it is simple to exaggerate or overlook certain authors. Montesinos, Le Gentil, and Berkowitz prefer to tie Mesonero to Cervantes, Mercier, and Jouy respectively.

It is also common to carry enthusiasm for sources too far. For example, some have said that Mesonero owes his good humor and amiable style to Jouy (Berkowitz), while others suggest Eugenio de Tapia (M. E. Porter). It seems trite to observe, but possibly Mesonero owes it to no one. Why does it have to be a literary inheritance? Must everything be based on a model? Mesonero's contemporary critics agree that his style is a direct expression of his own personality.[20] Don Ramón suggests the same thing repeatedly.

A similar point could be made regarding Don Ramón's tendency to moralize through satire. Many "sources" from national and foreign literatures have been adduced including La Bruyère, Courier, Mercier, Addison, Clavijo y Fajardo, Quevedo, and

Zabaleta. Again, to single out one or another and not take into account a long tradition in this vein is to distort the picture. Also, Mesonero's entire life, dedicated as we have seen to social and material reform of Madrid, is not out of harmony with his *costumbrista* irony and satire. The latter is merely an expression of the man, and his recognition of national defects.

However, within the framework of the national and foreign currents which have been elaborated in the preceding pages and remembering the significance of the writer himself—his own originality and evolution—there are definitely specific models that can be suggested for many articles; some of these will be pointed out in the following analysis of the *cuadros*. For now, only a few summary statements will be made.

Berkowitz has minutely demonstrated that Mesonero owes Jouy a large debt in style, themes, and techniques. Even so, it can be argued that on several occasions this scholar reaches exaggerated conclusions. At one point he contradicts what nearly every commentator—native and foreign—has said about Mesonero's truthful observation by implying that he has done no more than transfer the life of Paris to Madrid. On another occasion Berkowitz boldly states: "Indeed, Mesonero's sole claim to originality, generally speaking, is the skill which he frequently employs to conceal his lack of originality."[21] However, Berkowitz does recognize that Don Ramón outshines Jouy with a more animated, humorous style and more dramatic structures.[22]

Nearly every commentator before and since this study has agreed about Jouy's presence. Larra was one of the first to affirm this source; he stated in 1836 that Mesonero was a successful imitator of the Frenchman, but that the Spaniard was more of a thinker, less superficial.[23] None of this should be surprising since Mesonero repeatedly referred to his readings of Jouy. Berkowitz does not do justice to Mesonero's honorable recognition of his source. Besides frequent direct admission in his prologues and notes, the Spanish author at times specified within certain articles that the original idea was from Jouy. In *El aguinaldo* (*The Christmas Gift*), Mesonero dedicates the first paragraph to summarizing a similar article by his French counterpart. In *La casa de Cervantes* (*Cervantes' House*), another article Berkowitz credits to the Frenchman, Mesonero includes an epigraph from Jouy, one that captures the spirit of the forth-coming article. This is clearly an implicit bow of recognition as to source. This same kind of admission frequently extends to other sources. In a note to *El día de toros* (*Bullfight Day*), Meso-nero details his debt to Ramón de la Cruz.

In effect, Jouy's role should not be underestimated. Mesonero explicitly salutes this writer, states that he was moved toward *costumbrismo* by the Frenchman's influence, and often recog-nizes specific debts. If a fault can be found with Don Ramón, it would be that he later tried to minimize his debt. At times he suggests that he knew of his foreign "colleagues," but that he followed them only from afar. He also recalls in his old age that he tried to forget them as soon as possible, turning instead to national models. In this regard he mentions Quevedo, Vélez de Guevara, Cervantes, and others. F. C. Tarr concludes that this demonstrates that Mesonero was affected by the Romantic spirit of his times—i.e., the enthusiasm for temporally removed national traditions.[24]

The final disputable point relates to Mesonero's suggestion that until the Generation of 1830, the sketch of manners was not written in Spain, that he and Estébanez Calderón had com-menced something "absolutely new" (I, p. 39). This statement should not be misunderstood; by it Mesonero is referring to the *cuadro*'s precise form as developed through literary newspapers and divested of extraneous material. He is certainly not claim-ing to have invented *costumbrismo* since he repeatedly recalls the Spanish tradition in "...the festive painting of customs" (I, p. 40).

It is not difficult to know exactly which authors Mesonero esteemed. By examining his articles, prologues, epigraphs, and notes, one can compile a convincing list of writers to whom Don Ramón felt himself obligated. Further, in 1875 he published a lengthy index of his personal library. As a lifelong literary historian, Mesonero's own opinion must count. Having exam-ined this information, all of the extant source criticism, and the originals of most reputed models, I will present two lists, one for Spaniards, one for foreign writers. Since exhaustiveness is im-possible, I will limit my findings to significant influences on his *costumbrista* writings alone.

Spanish: Cervantes, R. de la Cruz, Vélez de Guevara, Zabaleta, L. F. de Moratín, Miñano, Cadalso, Quevedo, M. de Alemán, Salas Barbadillo, Castillo Solórzano, Santos, Liñán y Verdugo, Iriarte, Larra, Tirso de Molina, Fernando de Rojas, Espinel, Torres Villarroel, Eugenio de Tapia, Clavijo y Fajardo, Rubín de Celis y Noriega, Lucas Alemán, and Jovellanos. Also not to be overlooked is the large body of descriptive and critical articles and pamphlets (mostly anonymous) of the eighteenth century.[25]

Foreign: Jouy, Addison, Mercier, La Bruyère, Lesage, Courier, Monnier, Steele, Boileau, Molière, Diderot, and Montesquieu.

Furthermore, I would suggest that Mesonero Romanos was one of his own best sources. He reelaborates his material at different stages in his life, sometimes as many as three or four times per topic. Themes such as El Prado, El Buen Retiro, L. F. de Moratín; numerous types such as the job seeker and the flirt; most of his essays on literary criticism; and his guidebook-histories of Madrid, are sketched in his youth and more fully developed later. It is also common for his characters to reappear in various articles. Because of this and the fact that Don Ramón—within his *cuadros*—often refers to himself as a writer and to his previous similar articles, a feeling of an independent, coherent fictive world is produced, a feeling to be expertly created later by Pérez Galdós.

A final primary source which is often not recognized is the city of Madrid. The changing times, the contrasting parts of the city, the colorful human types all animate Mesonero's scenes, giving them a spirit not like that found in foreign models or those of a distant epoch. Don Ramón, in introducing the *Scenes of Madrid,* suggests that this work differs from the *Panorama* because of the changes in Madrid itself: "... it necessarily follows a bolder path and takes on stronger colors in order to sketch a new society, one produced by different laws, instincts, and tendencies than those which were exemplified in or which influenced the previous one" (II, p. 24).

Although sources for specific articles will be suggested in the later analysis, it seems fair to conclude that Mesonero's constant direct observation of his society, his passion for Madrilenian reform, his long travels abroad, his direct knowledge of Spanish and foreign descriptive writing, and his own roguish though amiable personality were together all equally strong factors in conditioning his style and vision.

IV   *Mesonero, Larra, Estébanez Calderón*

The best testimony of at least some originality among the major Spanish *costumbristas* is the notable disparity between the writings of each one. Montesinos, Ucelay Da Cal, Correa Calderón, indeed, all who treat these writers in comparative terms never fail to make vigorous contrasts.

Estébanez is generally alluded to as a regionalist (Andalusia) who was caught up in the spirit of the Golden Age. He employs archaic language, traditional rhetorical figures, recondite regionalistic and colloquial expressions, and emphasizes colorful types within a framework frequently similar to the short story. His intention is less social, more purely artistic than that of his colleagues. In this sense he can be compared to Juan Valera or to a modernist poet.

Larra, contrastively, is always remembered for his mordant wit, his increasing pessimism, his sharp psychological and cross-cultural insights, his preference for treating ideas and causes rather than outward manifestations of behavior, and his modern, cosmopolitan style. Larra is often referred to as a precursor of Ganivet, Unamuno, and the Generation of 1898.

The *costumbrista* who most influenced those that immediately followed was Mesonero Romanos. He can be distinguished from his contemporaries by his greater objectivity, his less penetrating irony, a conversational or chatty style, a fast moving parade of characters, and a frequent historical or erudite framework for his often moralistic sketches. This observable uniqueness seems tantamount to a partial negation of the imputation that these three—especially Larra and Mesonero—slavishly imitated Jouy.

In spite of these differences, there are also similarities which bind these three into what we may call the Generation of 1830. Ucelay Da Cal states: "... one notes in all three a reaction against the lack of historical realism in the Romantic novel, and the desire to reflect contemporary society with a certain truthfulness."[26] A budding realism, a reaction against escapism in literature, a classical sense of the moral "duty" of art are

to some degree all present—even though developed differently—
in these three major figures. Together they assert the independence of the sketch of manners, setting it entirely free of the
novel, the essay, and related forms. The *costumbristas* that follow, and they are legion, do not significantly alter the characteristics of form or content established by the Generation of 1830.

In any discussion of *costumbrismo,* the problem of priority
between Mesonero, Larra, and Estébanez Calderón is usually
approached. The stimulus for this discussion was the vanity of
these authors and some of their defense-minded panegyrists.
Pitollet suggests that Mesonero invented the sketch in Spain;
Cánovas del Castillo, a blood relative of Estébanez, argues that
the latter preceded Mesonero by months and Larra by even
more. Lomba y Pedraja indicates that Larra's work of 1828 in
El Duende Satírico del Día antedates all others.

The authors themselves, especially Larra and Mesonero, started
the controversy. Mesonero, apparently with a pricked vanity, responded to Larra's suggestion of simultaneous beginnings and
to another writer's assertion that Mesonero was a successful
imitator of Larra by reiterating throughout his life that he,
Don Ramón, began with Estébanez and preceded Fígaro by
months. A major difficulty is exactly what is to be called a
sketch of manners. Both Larra and Mesonero had published previously, the former in 1828, the latter in 1822. Neither referred
with frequency to these early writings nor used them in their
claims of priority. Apparently they were objects of embarrassment to each. Some later commentators prefer to disqualify these
early sketches on the grounds that they lack sufficient artistic
merit.

Many judgments as to priority have been based on these
authors' collaborations in *Cartas Españolas.* Estébanez published
several of his best known articles there in 1831. On January 12,
1832, Mesonero published his first sketch, entitled *El retrato*
(*The Picture*), in this same journal. Larra began his second
stage shortly after Mesonero. By this criterion, then, Estébanez
would precede his fellow *costumbristas.* However, many critics
now refer to *My Free Time,* Mesonero's work of 1822, as the
first collection of sketches by one of the three major figures. As

we have previously seen, this does not mean that Mesonero discovered this form in Spain.

V *A Writer's Creed*

Few Spanish writers of the nineteenth century have commented so frequently about their intentions, the nature of their genre, and their own artistic evolution as did Mesonero. Among the *costumbristas,* Larra may have made the most lucid remarks in his two part review of Mesonero's *Panorama of Madrid,* but Don Ramón, throughout his career, made many insightful observations in his prologues, notes, and even within his articles. The best sources for Mesonero's ideas are his article *Las costumbres de Madrid (The Customs of Madrid),* his preface to *Types, Groups and Outlines of Costumbrista Sketches* called *Adiós al lector (A Farewell to the Reader),* his prologues to the 1851 and 1881 editions of his works, and *Memoirs of a Septuagenarian.*

According to Mesonero, the purposes which moved him to *costumbrismo* were multiple. Although he emphasizes different motives from time to time, probably none is more repeated than the simple desire to call attention to the vices and absurd practices within his own society. From his first work in 1822 he insists upon this theme; later, in *The Customs of Madrid,* he observes: "A writer who proposes to attack the wrongs of the society in which he lives takes upon himself a grave and delicate responsibility" (I, p. 37). Many critics have not done justice to this aspect of Mesonero's work, preferring instead to concentrate upon the latter's traditionalism, patriotism, and good humor.

Following from the above, a second major purpose was to defend his nation against the distortions proliferated by works on travel impressions prepared by foreign observers. Angered by the superficial insistence on "romantic Spain," Mesonero sets out, in part, to give a more rounded picture. His observations usually, but unfortunately not always, go beyond the siesta, the bullfight, the midnight guitar serenade, and the gypsy dance. He summarizes concisely the almost paradoxical nature of his endeavor: "... where at the same time that we attack error, we also avenge the national character from the exaggerated insults, from the extravagant caricature in which its antagonists have presented it" (I, p. 39).

A third consideration was Mesonero's view that European society had moved into a new epoch, that change was rapidly occurring and would continue. He saw his beloved Madrid becoming more like other cosmopolitan areas due to improved transportation, increased travel, more mutual interdependence, wider education, and even the prior military invasions of Spain. A deep sense of history prompted Mesonero to sketch the old Madrid so that future generations would have knowledge of their roots. He was less interested in the great events of history than the more trivial quotidian episodes. Also, this author was not inspired by much of modern transfiguration; his use of the word "disfigure" to characterize the change is illuminating. As an older man he lamented the difficulty of sketching such a rapidly changing society.

A fourth motive can be found in Mesonero's honest acknowledgment of his positive reaction to a new literary style recently developed abroad. He states that he desires to initiate in Spain what Addison, Jouy, and others have successfully accomplished elsewhere.

Finally, we should not overlook an aspect rarely touched upon in this regard: Mesonero was an innate observer and commentator. While yet a teenager he was writing sketches and epigrams about his surroundings; also, his early documentation for the *Memoirs* clearly demonstrates this quality. At one point in the *Scenes of Madrid* he states that his mission was to paint the common man's day-to-day existence with an agreeable style (I, p. 40).

Throughout abundant references to his art, Mesonero commonly links his genre with his own personality. It is apparent that he identified closely with the sketch of manners, seeing in it a malleable form, one that suited his "humble" nature and "limited" capacities. Considering his typical statements about the genre, it becomes clear that most of them apply to the manner in which he alone employed its possibilities; they do not have the ring of an all-encompassing definition.

Nothing is more essential to the sketch, as Mesonero saw it, than the truth of the image and the moralistic purpose. When not presenting the facts or serving as a force for higher ethics, the *cuadro* was not functioning properly. The task of the "critic-moralist" was to chastise vice, praise virtue, and cast aspersions upon absurd behavior. Criticism, irony, benevolent satire are keys to this writer's view of his literary form. In one article he refers to his perspective as his "moral observatory" (II, p. 9).

Related to the above is the notion that all criticism should be done amiably, impersonally, indirectly. Mesonero never tires of affirming that he was a painter (using happy but pale colors), not a photographer. He drew types and figures, not individuals— a trait which aided him in communicating without offending. Just as important to Don Ramón was to avoid any political controversy. Apparently chastised thoroughly in his several bouts with the censors around 1830, Mesonero repeatedly disclaims political intention (even when clearly present in his writings), and refuses to publish his works in anything but literary and art journals.

A third trait is the *cuadro*'s far-reaching vision. Mesonero compares himself to the lame devil of Vélez Guevara; his observant gaze will be found in the darkest corners, in every district of the city, inside or outside. To give a complete picture is paramount, and to this end all classes of society should be on display.

Mesonero felt that a more permanent contribution could be made by concentrating upon that which might be called normal, tranquil, definitory. He saw that emphasis on the immediate and changing aspects of daily living would provide greater momentary popularity, but that his writings would soon be forgotten. It is not clear that Mesonero always followed this precept; in his writings there are numerous sketches of people given to stylish, modish living, although the perspective is one of amused irony.

In terms of form, Don Ramón often noted the *cuadro*'s brevity and simple dramatic framework, plus the interesting types of *castizo* ("pure Spanish") dialogue that give it animation. He felt the best sketches could combine aspects of the novel and the drama. Mesonero confessed several times his long-standing desire to write a novel such as *Gil Blas de Santillana;* he states that the changing times and his own recognized lack of capacity prevented him from doing so. With regard to his epoch, Mesonero went so far as to suggest that were Cervantes living in that moment, he too would find himself obliged to publish short fragments in the periodical press: the public was entirely conditioned to a new rapidity and brevity in its life style.

Don Ramón was highly aware of his manner of publication, and its role in determining the nature of the sketch. The need for brevity, a pleasing style, and inoffensive scenes was a direct result of the employment of the newspaper and journal, both forms dependent upon a severely limited buying public. That Mesonero knew how to criticize and still please is witnessed by the successful duration of his *El Semanario Pintoresco Español*.

Summarizing these comments about Mesonero's art is his oft-quoted remark which touches upon many of the characteristics of his sketches: ". . . to write for everyone, in an easy style, without affectation or carelessness; to describe most of the time; to reason infrequently; to never cause tears; to laugh often; to criticize without bitterness; to applaud without envy, and to aspire, in short, not for the glory of a great genius, but for the reputation as a truthful observer" (II, p. 11).

From time to time Don Ramón enjoyed measuring his own literary achievements. For example, he esteemed the *Scenes of Madrid* (1842) more than his first major work, the *Panorama of Madrid*. Many critics have agreed with him, but a notable exception is José Montesinos. The latter argues that the earlier sketches are less verbose, pallid, and essaylike. Don Ramón, however, insists that he employed bolder strokes and took more liberties in the second work since society itself had changed, thus permitting such an act. In 1881, he looked back, insisting that his collection of 1842, compared to the *Panorama*, had more philosophical purpose, a more mature system of thought, a more lively style, and that the society described demonstrated more political movement and greater vitality.[27]

There is evidence that Mesonero had planned a third work based on regional types rather than solely those of Madrid. He also desired to give it greater dimensions than that of the brief sketch. He confesses in 1862, however, that he was unable to vary his course, and the proposed work remained an embryo.

At this point certain critics habitually accuse Don Ramón of a lack of imagination or of deep insights into human behavior. The proof adduced is the failure to write a novel. In any case, Mesonero was honored to contribute several articles and a large concluding section to *Los españoles pintados por sí mismos* (*The Spaniards in a Self-Portrait*), 1843–1844, a two volume collection of nearly 100 sketches, many of which deal with general Spanish types.

In his prologue to *Types, Groups and Outlines,* Don Ramón honestly recognizes that his youthful abilities have somewhat diminished. He asserts that his earlier achievements had more spontaneity and dramatic interest; all he claims for *Types, Groups and Outlines* is a greater philosophical purpose. Due to his increasing age and the deep societal transformations in progress, Don Ramón decides to cease his *costumbrista* sketches after 1862. Following this date, except for his *Memoirs,* the main body of his work is literary history, criticism, biography, and public service writings.

CHAPTER 3

A Few Tentative Steps

BETWEEN 1820 and 1830 Mesonero Romanos was engaged in self-discovery and preparation for the future. He participated in various activities ranging from the National Militia and his father's business to poetry, the theater, and literary scholarship. As seen, in 1822 he also published his first prose sketches, a form that he was to later consider most proper for his talents. These tentative literary beginnings will be outlined in this chapter.

I A *Poet Without a Vocation*

In his youth Don Ramón fervently desired to become a poet. His works, many of which he wrote in the 1820s, were frequently presented orally to his peers or improvised in their presence, usually eliciting a hearty laugh or a knowing nod. Mesonero attempted numerous styles, but found most success in lengthy, festively satirical poems published among his prose sketches; these will be treated with the latter in our analysis. With a few notable exceptions, these "poetic articles" are the sole works in verse that Mesonero willingly published. The principal body of his verse writings was published by his sons in *Some Unpublished Prose and Verse*, 1883, and in the second volume of *Uncollected Works*, 1905. Don Ramón's *Memoirs* also contain some verse as do certain editions of the *Scenes of Madrid.*

Mesonero's own comments regarding his poetic labors represent a rather precise evaluation of his work; they also demonstrate his desire to be a poet and his disappointment at not finding success:

"From your prose, Mister Miguel de Cervantes, we can expect great things; from your verse, nothing." Thus spoke a book dealer to the prince of Spanish writers, and this same notion, remembering always the inequality of the comparison, the writer of the *Scenes of Madrid* has applied to himself. And not because the latter ever lacked desire, especially in his younger days, to cultivate the languages of the Muses, . . . but because, in the midst of his numerous and painful attempts, he became convinced that he had not received from heaven that holy fire of inspiration and enthusiasm that can never be replaced in poetry with formal correctness, study, and the imitation of worthy models.

Much time, nevertheless, transpired before he [Mesonero] clearly perceived this truth and renounced his poetic aspirations; many average compositions struggled and managed to escape from his incorrect pen. And since the style of the times, classical and regulatory, dictated the proper qualities for each genre, endorsing for its participants the proper attire for each situation, he put on his sheepskins and grasped his cane so as to sing eclogues, idyls, and madrigals to the sound of the pastoral flute; he crowned his head with vines in order to burst forth in Anacreontics and ballads; with ivy and cypress to intone solemn elegies and dirges; for his odes he begged Apollo for poetic inspiration and heavenly fire, the sun for its warm rays, the moon for its silvery face, and the stars for their quivering resplendence; he arranged perfectly in fourteen lines a hundred very subtle concepts in carefully constructed sonnets; he martyrized his thoughts in untold glosses, *ovillejos, décimas,* acrostics, and couplets with broken verses. He sang of love, lamented absences, spewed forth jealousy, shed tears, and either sent forth insults or highly complimented the altars of more or less fantastic, prosaic, or material dames such as Phyllis and Corina. Until, as a more mature man, and after calm reflection coupled with a serious study of his own faculties, he recognized sorrowfully that in all those verses there did not exist any signs of real poetry, that is to say, of true originality or high-minded thought, of that sublime style that characterizes the creative and inspired poet; and so, after hanging in a corner his prosaic lute that he had mistaken up to that point for a golden and tuneful lyre, he picked up a match, placed it in contact with that pile of badly written verses, and threw them, or their ashes, in the garbage.[1]

These lines were originally published in 1851. Later, in his *Memoirs* of 1881, Mesonero changed some details of his more youthful account. In both cases he was apparently more concerned with communicating some generalities about his poetry rather than a specific commentary about manner of composition, chronology, and literary evolution. The flippant or casual tone of the entire section plus the concentration of figurative language makes these small inaccuracies seem unimportant in their context; however, these same authorial comments have traditionally been accepted as fact.

One example relates to Don Ramón's story about burning many of his youthful verses. This story has been repeated frequently, but no one has produced any evidence apart from Mesonero's own statement. This detail is important since it relates to the existence of a body of literature produced by a significant figure in nineteenth-century letters. Concrete evidence appears to disprove—at least in part—Mesonero's assertion. First of all, there is a minor inconsistency between the two accounts; in 1851 Mesonero says he burned the papers with a match while in 1881 he jokingly retracts that notion since, as he says, matches had not yet been invented. Much more importantly, Mesonero's sons, in discussing the scope of their father's poetry, not only do not mention the burning, but actually allude to an unknown text called *Borradores de los pocos años* (*Youthful Rough Drafts*).[2] By publishing from this text numerous poems—many of them trite and prosaic—these sons have done much to disprove their father's account of their fiery destruction. They state that more exist, but simply have not been included. Also, they add that the author had condemned them to "perpetual oblivion," but they demonstrate by their publication and their allusion to the existing manuscript that this did not mean total destruction. Possibly only some poems or one of several extant manuscripts were destroyed; it is also possible that the entire story was a figurative expression of his own displeasure with his poetry.

Chronology is also somewhat distorted in Mesonero's accounts. In 1851 he implies and in 1881 he clearly states that after resolutely turning to prose as his expressive vehicle (probably about 1832), he renounced poetry once and for all. In a strict sense this statement is false since Mesonero later produced some sparkling *costumbrista* articles in verse plus many other poems throughout the remainder of his life. It is likely, however, that after 1832 Don Ramón wrote less verse than previously.

In several other details we may compare the 1851 and 1881 accounts and note certain additions or omissions which seem significant. In 1851 he specifically acknowledges his dependence on poetic models; in 1881, now more sensitive to certain attacks on his originality, he decides to omit that reference. His pride is also evident in that he does not emphasize in 1881 his own personal desires to excel in poetry; rather, he attributes his work to a social stimulus—all his companions were doing it, so why not he? Further, in 1881 he states that his writings were as good as those of his friends; his humility has clearly been replaced by a certain pride and defensiveness.

Don Ramón's poetry can be divided into several groups. During the 1820s he composed numerous poems openly imitative of certain "classical" Spanish poets such as Fray Luis de León, Meléndez Valdés, Fray Diego González, and José Iglesias de la Casa. These poems are set in most of the genres common to Neoclassicism such as the ode, the sonnet, and the *letrilla* (a verse form with a recurring refrain, usually festive or satirical). The vast majority are unsuccessful imitations with routine phraseology and uninspired thematic development. This is the part of Mesonero's poetry which—at least in form—most closely approaches lyricism. However, he was generally unable to express personal emotion in verse, even when dealing with such themes as the death of a friend, loneliness, or the sorrows of an unsuccessful love affair.

Mesonero's dependence upon poetic models during his period of initiation in the genre parallels his use of Jouy and Mercier in his *costumbrista* prose: he follows closely for a period but soon finds his own way. In general, Don Ramón gave up most of his attempts at lyricism after 1826.

Mesonero also dedicates various sonnets and royal octaves to what might be called "public realities"; that is, verses written in honor of some living celebrity, some important civic occurrence, or in memory of the recently deceased. These poems, also mainly confined to the 1820s, at times contain the seeds of a personal lyricism, but generally are more externally oriented than those of the first group. They are full of mythological allusions, well-worn comparisons, and a noticeably artificial, high-sounding vocabulary. In this vein is "Vista alegre" ("A Pleasing View"), a long descriptive work written in royal octaves which celebrates the plush retreat of a certain Josefa Martínez de Cabrero. In this poem Mesonero demonstrates how difficult it was for him to see and feel nature directly. He explicitly compares the natural surroundings to human virtues, or contrasts them to certain urban vices—a trait which recalls his pragmatic, middle class mentality. Several sonnets in this group describe happenings pertaining to the royal family, but probably the best one laments the death of Leandro Fernández de Moratín, a writer always admired by Mesonero. Their value systems, including their moralistic approach to literature, coincided, as seen in the second quatrain:

> Truth, soul virtue, philosophy
> weepingly kiss the bold hand
> that, with expert touch, knew
> how to oppose the attractions of vice.

> (Verdad, alma virtud, filosofía
> besan llorando la atrevida mano
> que con diestro pincel al vicio insano
> sus bellos rostros oponer sabía.)[3]

Another series of poems—all in a satirical vein and usually written in a burlesque, festive tone—are more difficult to place in time; many of them carry no date of composition. From the existing dates, it seems Mesonero was more steadfast in his cultivation of this genre. He normally employed the epigram, the *letrilla*, or the ballad for these relatively brief works. Principal themes are general human foibles such as avarice, lust for power or carnal pleasure, pedantry, and other ostentation common to nineteenth-century Spain.

Basic in Don Ramón's more lengthy poetic satires is a vision of mankind's moral unpredictability. Mesonero comments with ironic humor upon man's lack of steadfastness, dedicating one stanza to each example and repeating a catchy refrain intermittently. The tone is never too bitter. Common to these works is a final strophe in which the poet lessens his indignation, expressing the impossibility or even the undesirability of change. Moral distance exists between the poet and his created world during the body of the work, but it closes somewhat at the end. This moral reversal is in itself a reinforcement of the main theme of corruptibility, and also contributes to Mesonero's goal of never offending anyone as he teaches. Possibly the poem that best represents this aspect of Mesonero's work is "No sé si me explico" ("I Wonder If I Have Explained Myself Clearly"), a *letrilla* which expresses a view of an unstable world, of man's corruptibility, and of the poet's final compromise with these conditions. In another excellent poem, "La Cuaresma" ("Lent"), Don Ramón laughingly demonstrates man's hypocrisy during the season's religious observances; however, in this case, his irony is unrelenting through the final strophe.

Mesonero often turns the spotlight of irony partially or wholly upon himself, depicting certain personal feelings such as his desire to remain young, or mocking his own lack of social spontaneity or even his lack of poetic genius. The presence of this autobiographical element in his verse is so noteworthy that we may consider these as a separate group of works. It appears that Mesonero recognized his prosaic temperament even at eighteen years of age, for in 1821 he caused the god of poetry to say:

> You should write, my son,
> an unadultered prose,
> because, as long as I live,
> you will never be a poet.
>
> (Hablar puedes prosa neta,
> porque, hijo, lo que es poeta
> no serás viviendo yo.)[4]

The few poems preserved from Mesonero's last years are also partially autobiographical, and insist on the theme of the correlation between the poet's advanced age and his lack of poetic inspiration:

> From an untuned and
> largely forgotten lyre,
> do you strive to hear, my lady,
> sounds which it has now forgotten?

Not in vain do the years pass,
freezing all inspiration
and changing even the sweetest
nightingale into a buzzing horsefly.

(De una lira destemplada
y arrumbada en un rincón,
¿pretendes oír, señora,
sonidos que ya olvidó?
Que no en balde pasan años
helando la inspiración
y trocando en abejorro
al más dulce ruiseñor.)[5]

A poem written in 1881, one year before Mesonero's death, offers proof of his lack of real literary evolution, and serves as a partial summary of all his poetry. Echoing sentiments expressed in verse some sixty years previously, Mesonero, in "Los dos sietes" ("The Two Sevens"), constructs a two part work; at the outset he insists upon the theme of his lack of poetic talent, and, in the second part, he again creates an example of human hyprocrisy and weakness. His vehicle is Don Blas, a political philosopher who can say nothing but evil about Madrid until he finds personal gain in reversing his views:

But Don Blas ran across
some times that were good,
and so, what do you think?
There was one philosopher *less*
and one courtier *more*.

(Pero tropezó don Blas
con un lote de los buenos,
y resultó . . . ¿qué dirás?
Que hubo un filósofo *menos*
y hubo un cortesano *más*.)[6]

As a poet Mesonero was usually more audacious than as a prose writer. He makes erotic suggestions in verse, for example, that would seem out of character for him in prose. It is quite possible that his amorous youthful poetry embarrassed him later. Even in *El paseo de Juana* (*Jane's Stroll*), written in 1824 but published in 1832 as a sketch of manners, he boldly describes a prostitute's charms, her encounter with a young man, the presence of her steady "lover" and go-between, and suggests the possibility of venereal disease at the conclusion. Later in his life, a more frank communication is also noted within his verse, but usually in a moral, social, or political direction.

Mesonero frequently employed popular songs, refrains, and poems (his own or those of others) to give atmosphere and a sense of living history to his writings. This use of poetry for documentation and creation of setting is one of the most visible techniques in the *Memoirs.*

Even after relinquishing as a youth the strophic forms most related to Neoclassicism, Don Ramón continued to cultivate a poetry dominated by reason, pragmatism, irony, satire, and external realities. Narrative and description always predominate over lyricism. He is usually verbose and repetitive to a fault except in the epigrams. Just as with the prose sketches, the principal source of enjoyment is the good-humored ironic language, revealing an observer with whom it is easy to identify.

II My Free Time

In 1820, at seventeen, Mesonero read three pamphlets which described some of the political and journalistic celebrities of the day. He later affirmed that these sketches written by Azaola, Gallardo, and Gorostiza directly influenced his own literary beginnings. After receiving encouragement for his prose descriptions of some companions at the Belluzzi dance academy, he launched a more serious effort which was published in 1822 with the title *Mis ratos perdidos* (*My Free Time*). The earlier series of prose portraits was never published and seems definitely lost.

My Free Time is a brief work of twelve articles which also includes a preface and a final "Profession of Faith." In it Mesonero portrays a certain custom or scene considered typical for each month of the year. The work commences with October,

1820, and passes successively through twelve months, ending
with September, 1821. Most often the scene is related logically
to the accompanying month, but on several occasions the re-
lationship seems tenuous. The external structure is as follows:
October, the renewal of evening social gatherings (*tertulias*);
November, patriotic societies; December, Christmas season;
January, an elegant dance party; February, the theater; March,
a day downtown (*Puerta del Sol*); April, lawyers and courts;
May, the Saint Isidore celebration; June, bureaucrats at work;
July, the bullfights; August, a day at the park (*El Prado*); and
September, the marketplace.

In the *Memoirs* Mesonero relates an anecdote regarding
the original manuscript of *My Free Time* which several
critics have suggested is false. The author states that he lost
the entire manuscript one night while desiring to show it
to his friends. Fearful that the finder would attempt to publish
it under his own name, Don Ramón advertised the loss in the
Diario de Madrid. After no reply was received, he states that
he rushed to reproduce his work from memory, doing so in
only one night. Following this, he hurried to the publisher
with the finished product, still fearing the surreptitious publication of his lost papers.

This unconvincing story accomplishes three things. It continues Don Ramón's habit of carefree comment about some
of his literary experiences (another example was seen relative
to his poetry); it suggests praise for his perfect memory (a
main theme of the *Memoirs*); and it alludes to the circum-
stantial nature of his motives for publication. Since in later
life Don Ramón was thoroughly embarrassed by his first work,
too ashamed to even mention its title in his *Memoirs*, this
anecdote cleverly suggests he hurriedly published it in an
imperfect state for self-protection rather than for any notion
regarding its merit.

My Free Time was more recently involved in another un-
usual circumstance. As suggested above, Mesonero felt embarrassment over this early work. In effect, his own contemporaries of the post-1832 period do not seem remotely aware of
its existence. Don Ramón never based his claims to precedence
in *costumbrismo* upon *My Free Time*, something he easily could

have done and which critics often do today. This work was discovered and republished by the French hispanist Foulché-Delbosc in 1920.[7] Since the book was originally issued anonymously, this critic, unaware of its author, employed it to attack Mesonero's claims and to impugn his integrity. He suggested that many direct sources for the *Scenes of Madrid* are located in *My Free Time,* and that Mesonero boldly copied its motifs, style, tone, and structure in later writings. The Frenchman went so far as to claim that the 1822 work was superior to anything Mesonero later wrote. After this article went to press, Professor G. T. Northrup demonstrated to its writer by means of the *Memoirs* and the *Uncollected Works* (three sketches of *My Free Time* are reproduced there by Don Ramón's sons) that Mesonero was the author, and that, if he plagiarized, he plagiarized himself. Inexplicably, Foulché-Delbosc allowed his aggressive article to be published, attaching a postscript in which he acknowledged all of his misstatements.

Together the introduction and epilogue of *My Free Time* set the work's premise, vaguely introduce the narrator, and fix the tone by scathingly criticizing many of Madrid's customs. In these essays Mesonero attacks more bluntly than he normally did later. Subtle irony is not yet a tool the writer commands. In the introduction we read, "Because, who can indifferently contemplate the fact that in our times bad manners are taken as elegance, pedantry as learning, coquettishness as charm, a carefree attitude as a delightful personality, and, in short, that every vice is disguised with the name of a virtue? I, at least, cannot tolerate it, and, in a fit of pique, have scribbled these imperfect lines solely in order to vent my anger ..." (I, p. 4). In effect, this work, similar to others of Don Ramón, does not defend Spain from its foreign critics; rather, it represents an ironical view of his generation's perversion of the traditional Spanish way of life, a perversion profoundly stimulated by blind imitation of foreign models. Also stated for the first time is an esthetic principle which Mesonero repeats throughout his life: his desire is to expose vice generally, not in particular cases or as related to specific individuals.

In this introductory section the narrator coyly maintains

his anonymity, but insists upon his natural inclination to observation and criticism. This scarcity of information is only slightly
amplified within the twelve sketches; in these we learn that
he is from a small, rather distant provincial city, and that he
has come to Madrid to continue a pending law suit. Ignorant
of big city ways and desiring initiation into the "elegant"
stratum, the writer makes a friend (also anonymous) who
will advise him and accompany him to dances, parks, bullfights,
and so forth. The conversation between the two forms a large
part of each sketch. Also, this repartee between a native and
nonnative Madrilenian will be a basic technique in numerous
costumbrista writings during the next decades. It allows ample
room for ironical comment upon and impassioned defense of
certain customs. It was also a common basic premise in
seventeenth-century *costumbrismo*. It has been written that
Mesonero always took the part of the native defender;[8] this
is not entirely true. In *My Free Time,* Don Ramón (or the
narrative voice) is the provincial boy who is shocked by
Madrilenians: he is on the attack.

Also central to most later *costumbristas* is the principle of
anonymity for the narrator. This anonymity soon becomes
partial, taking the form of pseudonyms such as "The Curious
Chatterbox." The function of this technique is to provide a
"distance" which allows certain ironical relationships to be
cultivated. It also aids in these writers' desire to generalize
rather than specify.

In the concluding "Profession of Faith," Mesonero slightly
withdraws more of the narrator's cloak, especially in the moral
dimension. The entire section consists of a partial moral reversal identical to those commented upon relative to his
satirical poetry. Mesonero writes that he has become so
well instructed in the cultivation of elegance that he now will
defend this way of life forever. In fact, he intends to sell all
his holdings and buy the latest French fashions. This change
of direction is, however, more apparent than real. It comes
suddenly, without preparation, and after many pages of scath-
ing irony and satire; the reader cannot help juxtaposing the
two views. Also, a not too subtle exaggeration by the narrator
in stating his reversal makes evident its playful quality. For

example, Mesonero writes that he will forevermore speak a French-Spanish dialect so that Spain may be rid of its barbaric language.

Mesonero will proceed in this manner throughout his literary career. Little evolution in terms of style and technique is apparent in his writings. Abundant criticism is offered, but he mitigates it by his playful tone, verbosity, figurative language, and ironical overstatements. Also functioning to this end are the confessions of his own weakness and even enjoyment of the same acts being criticized (also a stylistic trait of Larra), his statements as to the impossibility of changing human nature, and his partly playful moral reversals at the conclusion. Don Ramón softens the blow, but gives a true although mellow picture. He was able to keep and even entertain his readers while criticizing and teaching them. This was the secret of his fame, and the most difficult part of his art.

Space limitations prohibit specific commentary on each of the articles. Instead we will focus briefly on one, and let the work's basic characteristics be gleaned from our general statements.

The first sketch describes the desires of the newly arrived provincial lad to participate in the autumn renewal of the *tertulia*. After months of summer vacation, numerous Madrilenians enjoy returning to their evening social gatherings. The narrator seeks out a friend with societal connections and beseeches the latter to initiate him into the ways of elegance. The reader first sees the corporal alterations made in the interest of the proper physical impression. Shortly the pair arrives at the party where the formalities of greeting are observed. When the novice wonders why only the beautiful young hostess was greeted, he receives his first lesson in Madrid's customs. In high society the female dominates the male completely; this practice is carried so far that the male consort remains entirely in the background at parties. When the narrator learns that the husband of the hostess is an old "walking ghost," he can hardly contain his amazement. Several slightly unfortunate incidents follow. In one the youth is invited to play cards, is distracted by the open flirting all about him, and almost loses his money. Soon after, he is struck by the beauty of a girl; he cultivates her acquaintance to the point of feeling hopeful about their future relationship, but quickly loses her to another. After receiving good advice from another friend and making a few moral reflections about his experience, the writer joins his first friend and they leave the party at the scene's conclusion.

Several traits present in this article can be applied equally to the others in the collection. Already mentioned is the dual perspective of the experienced and inexperienced interlocutors, and the wordy, playful irony which is bolstered frequently by harsh criticism or philosophical moralization. Beyond that, there is an accumulation of rapid encounters or miniscenes which usually terminate negatively for the narrator, thus allowing him to moralize openly or imply judgment by his expressed shock at such customs. These misfortunes are never too serious so that they basically remain at the level of entertainment. Within these brief episodes a gallery of human types appears and soon disappears with little dramatic or psychological development. Surface behavior is described, but the moral reflections allow a certain penetration at times. In this sense, the early sketches of Mesonero can be compared to the *sainete* ("farce"). Several articles in *My Free Time* could easily be staged, and compete with the farces of Ramón de la Cruz.

For purposes discussed above, the narrator deliberately imparts an overall vagueness to his creation. He protects his anonymity, only revealing a few details when necessary. None of the guests at the party are given a name or more than a word or two of description. The human cast is in shadows, only filling necessary roles so that the ironic presentation may be made. Groups and categories of people are present, but not individuals; there is a sense of the general dominating the specific. Identification of characters is made by such words as young girl, dame, gentleman, and madame.

The temporal dimension is also diffuse. The narrator locates the action in October, 1820, but it is clear that a renewal of the *tertulia* season occurs every autumn—nothing would differ significantly in any other year. The date seems arbitrary. In a more profound sense, the reader notes a seesaw effect between the dramatic present time and an eternalized moral or philosophical time. Normally, after each minor encounter within the article, a statement with ethical overtones is interspersed. This creates a temporal as well as a philosophical distance, preventing too close an identification with the characters, setting, or action. In terms of space, we see no streets or other landmarks; the reader only knows that the action occurs in Madrid at an elegant home.

Besides direct censure or moralization, Mesonero makes use of several more subtle methods of expressing his displeasure with certain practices. At times he plants a friendly or sage bystander in the crowd who witnesses the spectacle, and who then offers a piece of sound advice which implies condemnation. In the *tertulia* sketch, this occurs after Mesonero is rejected by the young girl.

Another method is the rhetorical question, employed at times in the presence of others, at times while the speaker is alone. The sagacity of the question and the lack of response imply censure. Ironic exclamations planted within description or narration also effect the same result.

But Mesonero's most subtle technique appears when he asks his companion a logical question about the wisdom or morality of a particular custom, and then allows the latter to give a long-winded response. This response, the reader notes, satisfies the speaker and any bystanders, but its emptiness is perceived by the reader and the narrator. Usually the latter will accept the explanation with ironic language. In the above article, a perfect example is seen when the two discuss the matrimonial customs of high society. The strategic moral alignment of the narrator with the reader should be noted; this practice demonstrates the literary complexity which actually exists within these apparently transparent sketches.

The critical focus in *My Free Time* is most often upon bad manners, superficial elegance based on servile imitation of French styles, coquettishness, indolence, disorganization, and immoral, escapist drama. The narrator presents himself as a young man, but his moral severity communicates a vision, at times, of a much older person. Despite Mesonero's youth at the time of composition, on occasion he makes penetrating, balanced observations which foreshadow his best writing. In the sketch for July on bullfighting, he places himself squarely

on the side of progressive foreign nations; his language is
harshly ironic:

And after all that has been said, can anyone possibly deny the
wisdom in such a philanthropic institution [bullfighting]? Is there
anyone that can think that the tavern-keeper should be taking care
of his tavern and fleeing from vain luxury and ostentation, the
married woman watching over her home and keeping herself from
unbecoming conversations, the debtor seeking ways to pay his obligations and not spending the few resources he has on these spectacles,
the worker in his shop, the employee in his office, a father's son
fulfilling his duties, and the rogue keeping himself from seducing
feminine innocence? Can anyone be so obstinate as to desire to
demonstrate the barbarity that these spectacles unleash on our national
character, the setbacks that our agriculture must suffer, the fortunes
that are wasted, and a thousand other observations so insulting as
to seem uttered by a Frenchman? Let the latter folk amuse themselves with their theater, their balloons, their experiments in physics,
and other such nonsense. We Spaniards, gifted with more energy
and spiritual loftiness, can only find amusement in scenes in which
we see a man's life compromised, imitating in this the enlightenment of ancient days through that sage law that claims that everything that is old is good. (I, p. 26–27)

This long quotation is cited to balance the distorted picture
some critics have given of Mesonero. He was not always a
partisan of old Spain, or a critic of foreign mores.

Berkowitz has suggested that several of these sketches of
1822 were already influenced by Jouy. This does seem likely
with regard to "Saint Isidore" and "An Evening Social Gathering." It is also true that Mesonero used himself for inspiration
in that he returns later to reelaborate several of these embryonic
sketches into some of his most masterful *cuadros*. There are
clear similarities between "An Evening Social Gathering," "El
Prado," "Navidades" ("Christmas Season"), and "Academia y
ferias" ("Literary Societies and Market Days") of *My Free
Time*, and *Las tres tertulias* (*The Three Parties*), *El Prado*,
El aguinaldo (*The Christmas Gift*), and *Costumbres literarias*
(*Literary Customs*) of the post-1832 period.

Finally, although each of these sketches is related to a
loose principle of narrative unification, the connection is so

slight that if one disregards the preface and epilogue, each article seems quite independent. This is clearly a departure from the tighter narrative structure of the picaresque novel or the guidebook of Madrid. These *cuadros* are also significantly more brief than the usual *costumbrista* pamphlets of the eighteenth and early nineteenth centuries. The latter frequently more resembled a political or ideological tract than a description of contemporary customs. No claim as to originality of genre is made for Mesonero, but it is obvious that *My Free Time* does move the sketch of manners closer to its definitive nineteenth-century form. We must not forget that Mesonero also published a number of individual *cuadros* in 1822. In this study, these are grouped among his miscellaneous works.

III *An Attempt at Drama*

The restoration of Ferdinand VII in 1823, with the following years of strict censorship and limited access to publications, caused Mesonero to turn to study and to his business affairs. From 1824 to 1826 he completed his literary education, concentrating upon seventeenth-century drama. Don Ramón's interest in this epoch is genuine, but his vision is deeply colored by his adherence to Neoclassical doctrine.

Mesonero wrote only one original play, and it was never staged. His efforts were principally directed toward the restoration of the national drama by means of adaptations of Golden Age plays. These *rifacimenti* were common in Spain during this period. Dionisio Solís, Cándido María Trigueros, Vicente Rodríguez de Arellano, and Félix Enciso Castrillón, among others, had been for years successfully "bringing up to date" numerous works of Lope de Vega, Tirso de Molina, Calderón, and others.

Between 1826 and 1828 Mesonero staged five adaptations, three by Tirso de Molina, one by Lope de Vega, and another by Antonio Hurtado de Mendoza. At times Mesonero modified the titles; at others he did not. The three plays by Tirso were *Amar por señas* (*To Love by Signs*), *Ventura te dé Dios, hijo* (*May God Grant Thee Fortune, Son*), and *La dama del olivar* (*The Lady from the Olive Grove*). In Don Ramón's hands the first became *Es una de las tres y de las tres no es ninguna* (*It Is One of the Three and of the Three It Is Not Anyone*), and

the third *Lorenza la de Estercuel*. The latter was a risqué
comedy with an untranslatable title. Mesonero's sons reproduced all the adaptations except the latter in volume two
of *Uncollected Works*. For their one omission, they pleaded
the cause of modesty.

From Lope de Vega, Mesonero took *La viuda valenciana*
(*The Valencian Widow*), and from Hurtado de Mendoza,
El marido hace mujer y el trato muda costumbre (*Husbands
Fashion Their Wives and Experience Changes Habits*). The
latter was never staged, and in later years Mesonero admitted
it had little merit. His adaptation from Lope was a large
success; it ran for twenty days and returned to the stage some
nine years later.

Don Ramón also translated from French a play by Mazères,
Marido joven y mujer vieja (*A Young Husband and an Old
Wife*). This work was staged at the Príncipe Theater in 1828.
The previously mentioned dramas alternated between the
Príncipe and the Cruz, the two principal theaters of Madrid.

Mesonero apparently enjoyed a good relationship with a
group of well-known actors. From partial knowledge regarding
his casts, it is known that each play was usually represented
by the same players. The principal members were Joaquina
Romea, F. Romea, Rafael Pérez, Antonio Guzmán, J. Tamayo,
Antera Baus, Teresa Baus, Pedro Cubas, and José García Luna.

The basic criteria underlying Mesonero's adaptations respond
to his concern for formal regularity and public morality. Without detailing differences between the original work and Mesonero's version, we may conclude that normally Don Ramón
eliminated nonessential characters and actions, condensed the
temporal and spatial dimensions (frequently stretching these
three act plays to five in order to accommodate place changes
to an entire act), and moderated salty language and embar-
rassing allusions.

The degree to which Mesonero altered the original text
varies in each case, although the criteria remain unchanged.
The fewest modifications were made in *To Love by Signs* and
the most in *The Lady from the Olive Grove*. The adaptation
was not always merely a matter of pruning or a new arrange-
ment of the parts. In *The Valencian Widow* the fifth act is

almost entirely original; in *The Lady from the Olive Grove* Mesonero rewrote an incident so that a clergyman took as his tithing the one daughter from a poor farmer with nine sons and one daughter. Later, the censor forced him to change the daughter to one of the sons, so Mesonero published the first version as a separate poem. When he added verses or made substantial alterations, Mesonero took great care to imitate the flavor of the original style. His success can be easily measured by comparing texts.

Mesonero's only original full length play was entitled *La señora de protección y escuela de pretendientes* (*The Influence Peddler and Her School for Position Seekers*). Written in 1827, this youthful attempt at a Moratinian comedy of manners was never staged because of objections by one of the censors. Believing that certain allusions would be inconvenient, the censor recommended modifications which the author refused. Mesonero felt that the play already suffered from an "extreme paleness" (I, p. 133), and that any further weakening would destroy it. Although his view of the play's particular weaknesses was not in agreement with that of the censor, Mesonero did suggest later that he was happy that the work was never staged, due to its lack of merit.

The Influence Peddler dramatizes the intrigues of an ambitious widow (Ursula) who provides for herself and her beautiful daughter (Manolita) by promising newcomers to Madrid that she can obtain government positions for them with her influence. In her dealings she works with a rogue who plays the part of influential men by using disguises and a quick wit. The widow collects "expenses" frequently, thus turning a good profit. The conflict centers on Ursula's desire for Manolita to marry one of the vain and elderly pretenders while Manolita is already in love with the young, handsome, virtuous Luis. Fortunately, Claudio, Ursula's brother, intervenes to arrange the affair so that the guilty are lightly chastized and everyone's wish is granted.

This play tightly observes all Neoclassical tenets of unity. Composed of only two acts, the action occurs within a few hours in a single room. No secondary plots or characters interrupt the flow, and no undue changes of tone can be found.

The exposition appears complete at the beginning; no attempt is made to disguise any of the parts. Unity is so important to Mesonero that he monotonously composes the entire work in the ballad form: the first act with a-o assonance, the second with e-a. The only exceptions are two brief morality stories which Mesonero had apparently composed previously and then interpolated in this play. These parables are written in *quintillas* (stanza of five verses, each with eight syllables) and *redondillas* (stanza of four verses, each with eight syllables); the concluding strophe of each conveys the moral.

The Influence Peddler offers a perfect example of obedience to formal precepts without underlying dramatic talent or inspiration. Mesonero recognized this honestly, and immediately ceased his efforts as a playwright. In this work the characters are only caricatures of vices and virtues; possibly the most offensive is the "kind" uncle Claudio. Without the numerous coincidences and unmotivated stage entrances by the characters, there would be no conflict or resolution. The only glimpses of psychological content are gleaned through conventional but undramatic soliloquies and asides. Mesonero later based one of his most successful *costumbrista* sketches, *Pretender por alto* (*To Start at the Top*), upon this play. His own description of his temperament as prosaic seems amply proven through his experiences with poetry and the theater.

Although most of our comments regarding the literary scholarship of Mesonero are reserved for a later chapter, one aspect seems pertinent here. In 1828, Don Agustín Durán published his landmark discourse on Golden Age drama in which he maintained that critics steeped in Neoclassicism had wrongly denigrated one of Spain's national glories by using inapplicable criteria. Durán's arguments denied validity to the efforts of those who modified the works of Lope, Tirso, Calderón, and their followers. A host of articles on both sides of the polemic were published. Even Mesonero replied in defense of reasonable adaptations, but he soon relinquished his position as Durán's arguments and the growing tide of Romanticism made headway. Don Ramón never again adapted the works of others, and even reprimanded others for doing so in his later years. Between 1857 and 1861 he edited five volumes of early dramatic works for the *Biblioteca de Autores Españoles* (BAE). He respected the integrity of the texts in each case. His affinity for Tirso developed greatly over the years; the latter was the subject of critical discourses and a special anthology by Don Ramón.

CHAPTER 4

A Life of Literary Activism

MESONERO'S writings dedicated to his native city, and, by extension, to the welfare of its inhabitants, are numerous and varied. Generally these are works of information or propaganda, only approaching imaginative literature in certain inspired passages. For this reason, even though they are well written and vital to an understanding of their author, our reference to them will be brief.

Mesonero's public service writings cannot be linked to any particular period of time: they cover his entire adult life. Their reformist nature is a product of his trip to France and England between 1833 and 1834, but his first book on Madrid had already gone through two editions before that date.

It is possible to separate these writings into three divisions according to their temporal focus. His landmark *El antiguo Madrid (Ancient Madrid)* of 1861 is dedicated to the past. This is truly an impressive work, one that culminates a long life of research, observation, and writings. Pointing more to the present is the *Manual de Madrid (Manual of Madrid)*, a popular work somewhat resembling a guidebook which went through four editions—extensively rewritten each time—between 1831 and 1854. The research for the *Manual* began in 1826, a fact which demonstrates Mesonero's lifelong concern for his city.

The future of Madrid was Mesonero's most pressing preoccupation. In spite of some critics' attempts to promote a vision of a backward looking *costumbrista*, Don Ramón gave the bulk of his energies to inspiring change and improvement. His unceasing journalistic and personal efforts to this end are a testimony to his progressive nature. In fact, Seco Serrano has recently struck a new chord by complaining that Don Ramón was too committed to modernizing Madrid: he pushed at times for change even at the expense of the city's most deserving traditional sites.¹

Past, present, and future, then, are all included in Mesonero's efforts to make his compatriots more mindful of civic affairs. The above division, though, is not meant to be rigid. Mesonero frequently presents an historical perspective in his writings; also, his enthusiasm for progress is not usually contained even when he is principally concerned with the past or a descriptive account of the present. To some degree, all three temporal viewpoints are normally blended into his writings.

I Manual of Madrid

Emilio Cotarelo has produced a lengthy review of books which describe Madrid previous to Mesonero's *Manual*.² From it we may conclude that earlier efforts had been partial, and by 1831 were wholly unsatisfactory due to the many changes in the city's physical circumstances. The most useful source was the anonymous work of 1815 entitled *Paseo por Madrid o Guía del forastero en la corte* (*Stroll Through Madrid or Guidebook for the Foreigner in Madrid*). It appears that Mesonero took some ideas as to the organization of his materials from this source.

Don Ramón's *Manual* was concluded by December 10, 1830. However, publication was delayed for almost one year because of difficulties with the censor. Since the *Manual* contains no sensitive political or religious materials, the long delay does seem ludicrous. Jean Sarrailh penetrated to the core of the problem by consulting city documents.³ Several days after Mesonero presented his manuscript to the Council of Castille, he received a denial. Flabbergasted at such action, he petitioned the council, and visited many of its members. In so doing he discovered that the council itself had never seen the work; a lowly subordinate who had formerly worked at the Latina Hospital had read only the section concerning the hospital, had found several errors of fact, and, on that basis, had condemned the work as inaccurate. Don Ramón then convinced the Council of Castille to deliver the manuscript to a committee of the City Council. In April of the following year, Mesonero learned that these bodies had given unanimous approval.

Since his father had been a business agent for out-of-town

interests, Don Ramón, even as a young child, could recognize the need for a guidebook of Madrid. This recognition was fortified after 1820 when the author himself had to deal with disoriented newcomers. Mesonero also had other motivations impelling him. After his lack of real success in poetry and the theater, he desired to gain a solid reputation so as to prepare his way in publishing circles. His honesty is refreshing in this regard: "... he [Mesonero] thought that it might be convenient to test it [his imagination] in a work that, though not lacking completely in literary qualities, could, because of its obvious practicality, attract the good will of the public to the author" (V, p. 182).

Mesonero's business acumen was not wasted in the successful promotion of his work He publicized his bouts with the censors to gain advance notoriety, he invested heavily in illustrations and a luxurious appearance for his edition, and he personally delivered a copy to high officials including King Ferdinand himself. Success was immediate. The first shipment to the bookstores included three hundred copies; they were gone the first day. The entire first edition was sold in several weeks. Congratulatory visits and messages arrived from the highest officials. The City Council opened its archives to him for further research, and a book dealer offered to finance a second edition. Don Ramón used this momentum to immediately begin publication of his sketches of manners. His success was now more assured. An understandable pride seeps through his account of these events: "... if Bretón's poetic genius was granted the glory of attracting people to the theater, my poor and prosaic wit was allowed not a lesser triumph, almost unbelievable in those days: to show the public the way to the bookstore" (V, p. 185).

One further repercussion of the *Manual's* success has apparently gone unrecognized in critical circles. A keynote in Spanish Romanticism is an enthusiasm for and cultivation of local, regional color. This insistence on picturesque detail carries over to the early novel of Realism, giving it one of its distinguishing marks. Mesonero's *Manual*, which details historical, anecdotal, and other aspects of Madrid, clearly foreshadows this trend. The significant aspect in making a case for his influence is the wide diffusion and great popularity of the *Manual*: the editors of the *Diccionario geográfico universal* (*Universal Geographic Dictionary*) of Barcelona extracted portions of it, and imitative manuals and guidebooks soon appeared in various provincial capitals. A new pride in the uniqueness of local and popular life may have been strongly stimulated by the success of the *Manual*.

The first edition of Mesonero's *Manual* contains an introduction and fourteen chapters. Seco Serrano has concisely summarized its contents by terming it "... an abridged history, a guidebook, and repertory of monuments."[4] Chapter 1 relates various theories as to the origins of the capital and its name, describes its arms and heraldry, and summarily discusses some of the most distinguished native sons. A disproportionate amount of space is given to Leandro Fernández de Moratín, always one of Don Ramón's special interests.

Chapter 2 describes Madrid's topography, climate, population, taxes, interior divisions, inns, methods of transportation, restaurants, system of coinage, and other matters pertinent to a newcomer. An interesting personal interpretation of the physical and moral character of the inhabitants is given: Mesonero praises their wit, social grace, and appearance, but laments their superficiality, servile obedience to foreign styles, poor education, lack of ambition, and weak physiques. A sharp critique is made of the lowest class, one which caused some negative reaction after publication. Don Ramón notes these people's lack of morality, slothfulness, violence, and deviousness. His hope is that good instruction may one day improve this situation. This confidence in education was apparently not all idealism. After spending the next thirty years dedicated to improving the life of the lowest class, Don Ramón could write in 1861 that "... it has made great gains in morality, in education, and in material comforts" (IV, p. 172). Some pet projects during these years were a savings and loan association for the poor; modern day care centers; new, liberalized pedagogical methods; and better schooling for the blind. He also attributed the improvement in their situation to political events, especially a growing class consciousness: recent political events had demonstrated that an organized stratum of society could influence the course of events. There was now more hope.

Chapter 3 is dedicated to government. The organization of the royal palace is detailed as are the various councils, ministries, boards, and administrative offices. In Chapter 4 Mesonero informs the newcomer about the judicial system, and in Chapter 5 he discusses the city's civil, military, and ecclesiastical organization.

Chapter 6 describes the seventeen parochial divisions, and then gives historical background for each of the seventy convents. Other religious edifices such as chapels and cementeries are included. Chapters 7, 8, and 9 introduce the reader to the central issues regarding welfare, the poor, hospitals, prisons, schools, museums, libraries, business, industry, and the arts.

Plazas, palaces, fountains, and other notable buildings are the subject of the next division. In Chapter 11 theaters, gardens, promenades, and other public diversions are described. This is undoubtedly the best written portion since it is given to the same general subjects that the author so successfully treated in his *costumbrista* writings. Chapter 12 is more utilitarian as it describes the entrances to the city, the canals, the river, the bridges, and the water supply. The next chapter gives information on the surrounding countryside, the various royal sites, and the nearby villages. The final chapter is a lengthy list of Madrid's streets with the entrance and exit point of each. Throughout the entire work, wherever pertinent, the author includes statistical tables, lists, and other data useful to a nonnative Madrilenian. Also, frequent and sometimes extensive footnotes supplement the historical background, provide colorful anecdotes, suggest related readings, and supply additional facts or statistics.

This first edition is well written and impressively documented, especially when one considers the youth of the author. The style is concise and direct, more so than in later years. A higher degree of impersonality is also in evidence, but it is not complete. Mesonero sometimes describes in an evaluative manner as with his treatment of the lowest social classes. Also, at times he lets his historical, architectural, and artistic preferences be felt. His condemnation of the late seventeenth century is strong. He rails against Pedro Ribera, José Donoso, and others of the churrigueresque school of architecture. Special praise is given to Philip II and Charles III, the former because he definitively located the Court in Madrid, the latter because of his contributions toward modernizing and beautifying the city. Mesonero is not abusive of Ferdinand VII since the king was still alive through the first two editions. He gives special recognition to this king's efforts toward the development of the Royal Museum of Painting and Sculpture. Also, even in the first edition, there are several strong objections to certain conditions in Madrid; one example is his plea for a more logical and systematic house numbering system. Mesonero would soon see this change effected.

The *Manual* contains lengthy descriptions of buildings—their exteriors and interiors—together with an inventory of their significant contents. The reader notes in these details an eclectic approach to public affairs. Mesonero is able to combine a desire for practicality and modernization with his equally strong wish for beauty. Even though his esthetic preference is clearly Neoclassic, he rarely condemns other manifestations unless they are in extreme "bad taste," or they display disregard for clearly superior options. His principal concerns were comfort, spaciousness, symmetry, and the always subjective "good taste."

II Later Editions

The second edition of the *Manual* appeared in 1833. Certain additions, modifications, and new illustrations added thirty-six pages to the text. Soon thereafter Mesonero left on a ten month tour of France and England, a trip which was to prove a key event in the author's life. He was able to make observations which stimulated his dedication to the improvement of his city.

During his absence many significant changes had occurred; these events had altered the organization, administration, and physical makeup of Madrid. A new constitutional monarchy was in power, one which gave increased responsibilities to the parliament. A civil war had erupted, and numerous convents and other religious institutions had been destroyed. Rather than completely rewrite his now out-of-date *Manual*, Mesonero opted for the addition of a two part *Appendix* which he published in January, 1835.[5] The first third of this work took into account the city's recent changes, and the remainder outlined the author's opinion of needed reforms. To give further impetus to these projects, Mesonero, in May of 1835, took under his personal control the *Diario de Madrid;* in this newspaper he publicized the city's needs, the prospects for change, and the actual reforms as they occurred. Also at this time, Don Ramón entered into a tacit partnership with the Marquis de Pontejos, the mayor of Madrid. Together this pair effected the majority of the changes Mesonero had propounded.

Since this *Appendix*, with its numerous ideas for improvement, suggests the line of thinking which Mesonero expanded in following years, I will briefly summarize its contents, not attempting to do so with later similar writings. It was divided into four parts, the first dedicated to matters of health, comfort, and beautification. In this section Don Ramón suggested reforming the municipal ordinances, taking an exact census for better planning, requiring all construction to meet a uniform code which would take into account symmetry and the welfare of others, expanding the city limits to the North and East, constructing covered marketplaces to replace carts and street corner vendors, using cobblestone for paving instead of pebbles and rocks, widening and regularly cleaning many streets, building new plazas and parks, reforming the house numbering system, and renaming many streets to reflect national glories of the past.

The second part suggested with detail new hospitals, asylums, a reformed *Monte de Piedad* (pawn shop), and the creation of a savings association for the poor. Part Three was dedicated to commerce and industry; in it Mesonero hoped for more modern restaurants and hotels, new life insurance societies, better urban transportation, the elimination of many holidays, and the suppression of bullfighting on working days. The final portion, Part Four, was given to education and recreation. Mesonero desired that the University of Alcalá be transferred to Madrid (realized the following year), and he proposed the creation of the *Ateneo* ("Atheneum"), new academies, museums, libraries, and neighborhood theaters. Most of these ideas were converted into reality, either soon after their proposal or during Mesonero's four year term on the City Council from 1846 to 1849. Many more worthy suggestions were also promoted in his newspaper articles, which began to alternate with his sketches of manners.

An expanded third edition of the *Manual* was published in 1844. Mesonero modified the organization of the material somewhat, added to the historical introduction, and brought the administrative, topographical, and artistic sections up to date. The net result was an addition of 110 pages. Throughout the course of these changes the work itself was undergoing a steady transformation, one that would culminate in the fourth edition. Instead of being principally a guidebook of information for the newcomer, the *Manual* was becoming a source for the native citizen. The increasing emphasis on history and the growing importance of the author's own interpretations and emotions regarding the city's characteristics constitute fundamental factors in this change.

The final version of the *Manual* appeared in 1854. Unfortunately, this was the year of a revolution in Madrid, and Mesonero's work, because of destruction and change, became somewhat outdated while still in press. Even though this edition utilized the same organization as the 1844 version, Mesonero gave it a new title: *Nuevo Manual histórico-topográfico-estadístico, y descripción de Madrid (A New Historical-Topographical-Statistical Manual, and a Description of Madrid).* Over 176 pages of new and more detailed material were added. Mesonero submitted that Madrid had changed so drastically that not a single page could escape revision. It is true, however, that great similarities continued to exist between all of the editions.

In the version of 1854, the evolution toward a book principally for the use of native inhabitants continued. Still more emphasis was given to history (especially that of the sixteenth and seventeenth centuries), and to national glories of the past. The author's subjectivity also increased, a fact which also makes the book more suitable for a native reader. For example, he condemns three centuries of public figures for their failure to modernize or beautify their city in accord with the possibilities of their times. Also, as he passed review over convents, churches, and other buildings formerly treated more dryly, he usually added his own views regarding their location, utility, or beauty. The description of San Francisco el Grande provides an example (italics mine): "The lobby of the church is sixty-seven feet wide and thirty-seven feet deep. On the building's front there are two towers which are *too small*, and three arched entrances. This temple, even though *it lacks embellishment* and *in spite of the defects* which critics can find in it, is the most imposing in the Court though *unfortunately* it is situated in an *out-of-the-way place*, that is, down from the Puerta de Moros" (III, p. 309).

Indeed, the structure of description has taken on a fuller, more literary quality in many instances. Neatly combined in numerous paragraphs is an objectivity of mathematical precision, a highly technical vocabulary, an historical sketch of origins and evolution, and an interpretative aspect usually based on utilitarian and esthetic grounds. Not lacking in many cases either, is a display of authorial emotion which at times borders on lyricism.

III *Other Civic Publications*

In 1846 Mesonero was elected to the City Council. He served for four years. During this time his activity apparently was unceasing to judge by the volume of work he accomplished. Several months after his election he published *Proyecto de mejoras generales de Madrid* (*Plan for General Improvements in Madrid*). This work was principally concerned with dissuading the government from proceeding with a full scale amplification of the city. Mesonero argued from historical and foreign precedent, used economic and population statistics, and presented an alternative plan—the latter a typical tactic of the author. Don Ramón proved convincingly that with modernization and new design, the present urban radius would be sufficient. His plan was adopted by the council, and later made governmental policy. Many new or wider streets, improved plazas, and other tangible results followed. For example, the Plaza Mayor was beautified, and, at Mesonero's petition, it was adorned with a statue of Philip III which Queen Isabel II gave to the city; the statue was previously installed at her Casa de Campo.

In 1847 Mesonero was charged with the reformation of the Municipal Ordinances. He soon accomplished this task, and saw his work accepted and published. In 1849, his final year of council service, he left the government a huge map of the city (126 square feet) and 600 other small maps of the individual streets. Plans for even more reforms accompanied these visual aids as did a new publication, the *Memoria explicativa del Plano general de mejoras* (*A Defense of the Plan for General Improvements*). This report, which can be consulted today in volume one of *Uncollected Works*, is interesting since it is partly given to summarizing many of the accomplished projects which Mesonero had originally proposed as well as those that were then in progress or not yet begun. The remainder represents further proposals and new justifications for completing his previous but unaccomplished ideas. Cotarelo sums up this portion of Don Ramón's work: "Since all these works have been reality for many years, many will find it difficult to believe that they were bold innovations during the middle of the past century."[6]

IV El Antiguo Madrid (Ancient Madrid)

Mesonero Romanos felt a lifelong affinity for the past, and for the weight of Spanish tradition. However, with his equally strong desire for social and material modernization, he was frequently caught in an apparent contradiction. Many of his proposed urban reforms required destruction or relocation of neighborhoods, streets, plazas, and monuments. The pick and shovel were especially integral to the realization of his ideas propounded in the 1846 *Plan for General Improvements in Madrid*. So that the past would not be entirely lost, Mesonero set out to capture it in detail by means of numerous newspaper articles and in the historical-descriptive accounts within his *Manual of Madrid*. This effort culminated in 1861 when he published *Ancient Madrid*, a work Sainz de Robles considers Mesonero's best.[7] Cotarelo affirms that "... it is a model in its genre, a work that has not been equalled by any other."[8]

Ancient Madrid, then, is a compilation and reorganization of many previous articles and portions of the various editions of the *Manual of Madrid*. There are also sections which were specifically written to fill lacunae in the above. The author recognizes in his opening remarks that an attentive reader will notice many repetitions if he is familiar with the past writings on Madrid. The newly written portions blend well with the previous articles—an uninformed reader would not notice the patchwork construction.

This lengthy work is divided into two parts. The first repeats the ever-present historical introduction to the founding and development of Madrid; the second describes the city according to its districts and neighborhoods throughout its various epochs. The historical overview, which makes up one-fifth of the work, is more extensive than in the *Manual of Madrid,* and more fully probes the sixteenth and seventeenth centuries. A solid effort at documentation has been made, based especially upon the *Plano topográfico de Madrid (Topographical Map of Madrid)* which was prepared in 1656 in Antwerp.

The second part is subdivided into four sections according to the original occupied territory of the city and its changes after the three succeeding expansions. These subdivisions are then further partitioned for purposes of exposition. Within each sector the author figuratively takes the reader by the hand, and amicably strolls with him from place to place. Anecdotes, history, statistics, and topography are pleasantly blended so that the image of ancient Madrid is vigorously presented. Above all, *Ancient Madrid* is filled to capacity with places, buildings, monuments, and objects. The most memorable stylistic achievement is the combination of erudition and readability. The "stroll technique" is vital to Mesonero's purpose, as is his own attractive personality which colors the potentially dry material. Emotion and exaggeration are not beyond the author as when he exclaims: "The *Puerta del Sol!* What citizen of Madrid, no, what Spaniard, even though he be in an extreme corner of the Peninsula or in the most distant reaches of our globe, does not feel interested, emotionally moved, at the memory of this name; what Spaniard does not embrace the idea of someday visiting this renowned site?" (IV, p. 209). Mesonero also warms the prose by adopting from time to time his chatty and racy *costumbrista* style. He explicitly recognizes this fact near the conclusion (IV, p. 215).

V *The Journalistic Effort*

The bulk of Don Ramón's progressive reformist activities can be found in his direct intervention into public affairs and in his newspaper work. This latter aspect, nearly continuous for thirty years, is difficult to treat in a brief study due to its heterogeneous nature and its great proliferation. Articles which can be called public service writings began to appear in 1822 in *El Indicador de las Novedades, de los Espectáculos y de las Artes,* and continued in at least ten different newspapers in the following years. The most important were the *Diario de Madrid* (which Mesonero directed in 1835), *El Semanario Pintoresco Español* (1836–1854), and *La Ilustración* (1850–1853). The author was still active in this effort through the last decade of his life, although these latter writings are more melancholic reflections than social activism.

Although Mesonero's sons published a sampling of these writings in the first volume of *Uncollected Works,* it is impossible to speculate on the precise contours of this portion of the author's work. Many articles which apparently are Mesonero's because of their subject and style are unsigned or carry slight variations on his initials or pseudonym. We can only guess, frequently, that they do belong to him. There are undoubtedly many worthy articles lying buried in these journals which would swell even more the already impressive bulk of Don Ramón's publications.

Mesonero's statement of purpose published in the *Diario de Madrid* summarizes well the diversity of this outward-oriented project:

. . . we will always strive to fill it [the newspaper] with statistical data about the capital, the changes in matters of public health, the industrial and mercantile activity of our city, the improvements in public sanitation, the progress in education, and other analogous subjects—at times directly presenting them to the public without commentary, at times taking the risk of adding our own pale observations. And, in order to make our task more pleasant, at times we will offer judgments as to the city's new obligations as well as diversions, gather together unpublished information and documents regarding the history of this city and its famous sons whether dead or alive, and present quick sketches of customs especially in order to point out new aspects of behavior brought on by the passing of time.[9]

Mesonero's travels, constant observation, and personal experiences gradually allowed him to fashion a public service philosophy which, after 1850, becomes the screen against which he projected all ideas for improvement. Earlier he seemed more guided by mere comparison with London, Brussels, and Paris. In an article of 1851 entitled *Mejoras de Madrid* (*Improvements in Madrid*), the author expresses the cornerstone of his philosophy.[10] An image of a tired public servant—one who now moves more cautiously—is not lacking in these words, but the article's content centers principally upon the need to reflect upon progress and tradition, and to consider practical matters such as space and finances. It also focuses upon the inadvisability of abstract idealism in matters of municipal reform.

As one reads Mesonero's newspaper publications, he is struck by the relative lack of negative criticism of the present, and the visible emphasis on concrete projects for improvement. Mesonero always had a plan. When in 1838 he proposed day care centers, he did not limit himself to a general description and an enumeration of advantages. Instead he described even the needed furniture, how the teachers would keep records, and how to teach even the youngest children useful things.[11] Don Ramón's practical mind focused on the detail and the minute; he also recognized the increased prospects for success when a plan was presented in a tangible form.

Mesonero dedicated his life to the past, present, and future of his native city. When all accounts are in, it was the future which most engaged his energies. Through his pages the reader can gradually see the transformation of a place. From a Moorish fort to a major European capital, each stage of Madrid's development is detailed in a style which combines erudition and intimacy, criticism and humor. As the account moves into the nineteenth century, it takes the form of a struggle, of a personal commitment. To Mesonero's credit, a high percentage of his dreams for the city became the realities of his countrymen.

CHAPTER 5

Escenas matritenses *(Scenes of Madrid)*

MESONERO Romanos' literary reputation rests principally upon the *Escenas matritenses (Scenes of Madrid)*. This lengthy collection of *costumbrista* sketches was first published as separate articles in diverse newspapers between 1832 and 1835. The author considers this journalistic appearance as the first edition. The original bound form consists of three volumes (two in 1835, one in 1838) entitled *Panorama matritense (Panorama of Madrid)*. In 1842 Mesonero added the articles written since 1836 and published principally in *El Semanario Pintoresco Español,* issuing all of them under the new title *Scenes of Madrid.* The original *Panorama* became known as the first series of the *Scenes of Madrid.* I will distinguish by name between the *Panorama* and the *Scenes,* as many still do today, only when convenient for expository purposes.

Apart from the youthful *costumbrista* antecedents studied previously, *El retrato (The Picture),* published on January 12, 1832, in *Cartas Españolas,* is known as Mesonero's first mature sketch of manners. With this article he first employed his pseudonym "The Curious Chatterbox," and also took his place beside Serafín Estébanez Calderón, a *costumbrista* who commenced his writings a few months earlier in the same journal.

In this chapter we will study as one unit both series of the *Scenes of Madrid,* leaving for separate treatment the author's final collection of sketches which was published many years later. Because of minor but frequent changes in the groupings of the sketches with each edition, I will employ the plan utilized by the author in the edition of 1881, an eight volume set of Mesonero's works, the first three of which contain his *costumbrista* articles.[1] This is the last edition that he directed before his death; in it he included previously written notes and added

93

several prologues. However, in order to provide continuity of reference, I will continue to cite from the most modern edition, an edition which contains all of the articles but which departs from the author's own groupings somewhat.

Since the 1881 edition of the *Scenes of Madrid* consists of seventy-one independent articles, it will be impossible to analyze or even summarize all of them. My comments will be directed instead to certain sketches representative of different themes, tones, and literary treatments. Previous to this discussion, I will offer my translation and analysis of an article entitled *A prima noche* (*In the Early Evening*), especially selected for its brevity and representative nature rather than for literary excellence alone.[2] My translation is based on the article as it appears in the edition of 1881. It is hoped that a close analysis of one typical article will partially compensate for the impossibility of treating each one on an individual basis.

I *A prima noche* (*In the Early Evening*)

It is generally believed, and one might say rightly so, that generosity is one of the distinctive traits of a Spaniard's character. We are generous, in fact, in the widest sense of the word, generous and even lavish in both our necessary and superfluous spending; as proof we may consider our national debt, our offices, our palaces, churches, and monuments. We are similarly lavish in our hyperboles and other assorted rhetorical figures, and proof can be easily found in our enthusiastic historians, panegyrical poets, and in all the harangues, expositions, and manifestations that we see every day, and that could, if they were gathered together, serve as a general and complete guidebook of proclamations for every country of the globe.

But in the midst of our lavishness, with nothing are we more extravagant than with our time, and there is nothing, in truth, that we know how to waste with more charm and fortitude.

The industrial countries have considered time as the most valuable capital of all. We, generally speaking, consume it as though it were a revenue earned from our very existence. The Spanish expression *"hacer tiempo"* ("to make time") means to waste it in any other language, and a rapid stroll through our capital (to where our nearsightedness limits us) would bear this out better than any printed discourse.

For example, what is that parasitic mob of unmoving loafers doing in the Puerta del Sol, interrupting the flow of the pedestrians, memorizing all of the billboards, looking at the clock, or listening to the blind man's song? They are "making time" so that later they can cross over to the other side and engage in similar work.

What is that effeminate dandy waiting for, that habitual adornment of an elegant shop on Montera Street, that component part of its show window, that letter of its store sign, and that trustworthy inspector of its business operations? Is he moved by some mercantile interest, or by the desire to make economic or moral observations? Nothing further from the truth than that: he is "making time" until a certain husband goes to his office so that he [the dandy] may run to console the latter's wife, who waits for him by "making time" on the balcony, or trying out a new wardrobe combination in front of the mirror.

The husband, meanwhile, is seated in his bureaucratic chair, trying out the steadiness of his hand with some bold doodling, sharpening his pencils, stroking the coals of the firepan in order to give them a pyramidal configuration, rolling cigarettes that he offers to his associates, and, as he smokes, dissertating in front of the window on such subjects as the state of affairs in the plaza below or the bullfights; this man is "making time" until the boss comes to scold the doorman, tie and untie bundles of papers, ring the bell, and "make time" until it is two o'clock so that he [the boss] can take his hat in hand.

What is that magistrate doing buried in his crimson armchair, his head on its back and his eyes turned to the ceiling? Is he meditating on a defense in which a lawyer with amphibological arguments has "made an hour of time" in order to martyrize his brain? Certainly not sir: he is "making time" until the doorman who was playing cards with his fellow lackeys might open the door with a burst, announcing, "Sir, it is time to eat."

What is that workman looking for as he lets his gaze wander from the ridgepoint of a roof, his mattock raised, and his other hand extended as if he were giving orders to his crew? By chance could he be inventing a more advantageous cut, a technique which might prove easier and that might save time and labor? Nothing further from the truth than that: his penetrating vision, passing over roofs and chimneys, fixes upon the Trinity Tower as he joyfully warbles the old ballad:

> Noon arrived, it was exactly noon,
> the clock was striking twelve,
> in León the exalted King Alphonse
> is dining with his noblemen.

With the first toll of the bell, he simultaneously heaves his mattock to one side and descends the scaffold as a man released from the cares of his job, running to join his beloved mate, who, seated in the sun at the doorstep of their home on Paloma Street, "makes time" until the stew is done, or until her mischievous little boy or sleepy cat fall into the fire.

At no time is this universal emptiness, this *dolce far niente* (as the Tuscan said) more perceptible than at twilight; it is not enough for our apathetic indifference to unwisely interrupt our daily work for the solemn operation of a large meal at three o'clock; not sufficient for our repose is the second night, improvised at siesta time, or the obligatory stroll which continues until daylight has vanished; it is necessary to waste even several more hours in a café, or seated around a billiard table, or running around aimlessly in the streets, or visiting in the shops of friends.

If, after all, these extremely important hours—since they are not utilized to attend academies and lyceums, or to engage in mercantile or artistic labors—could be employed to make gains in our social intimacy, not in that public and fictitious society—quarreling and pedantic—that is found around a punchbowl or a billiard table, but that pleasurable, intimate society that is found within the families that are our friends; that society in which we may be ourselves without running the risk of personal compromise or of offending anyone else; that lovable and unpretentious company, in short, that forms a true friendship, love, and also sweet, lasting bonds; if this could be so, then these hours of recreation could be considered wisely utilized.

We mock our ancestors because they stopped only briefly for refreshments at a soda fountain or a café, and then continued on home at dusk in order to welcome their true friends and spend a few hours engaged in delightful conversation or decorous games. It must be admitted that in the old Canosa or San Antonio de los Portugueses soda fountains they did not find marble tables, or crystal chandeliers, or mirrors, or counters as we find in our present-day cafés; the truth is that a narrow table and even narrower bench, a large open lamp with four wicks, a bell-shaped glass, and a little basket of buns were all the stimuli that those dark rooms provided; but, on the other hand, the drinks were excellent, the crowds were large, and the few moments that one spent there made any physical discomforts entirely manageable. Of course there they did not find newspapers to read, politicians with whom they could argue, men of letters to flatter, military men to fear, or juicy stories to gossip about; but, on the other hand, they did not make a man deaf with their endless squabbling, they did not learn bad manners, they did not fall into the habit of repeating uncouth phrases, they did not become saturated with the foul smell of tobacco, and, above all, they did not pitifully waste their time.

"Good evening, Mr. Curious Chatterbox."

"Good evening, Sir Pascual."

"What are you doing?"

"Writing."

"And, to whom?"

"To the public."

"An excellent correspondent, even though a trifle deaf; can one know what it is all about?"

"Take a look." And I passed him the paper while I "made time" as he read it by enjoying the taste of an excellent cigar. Oh yes! This little respite also gives me the opportunity to inform my readers that this new speaker was precisely the same Sir Pascual Bailón Corredera whom they already know if they have read my previous articles entitled *The Actors at Lent* and *The Old Cape.*

"All this is very fine," Sir Pascual responded as he returned the paper after reading it, "but who hired you as a censor of morals? Do you really think that there is anything more delightful than our early evening activities? Look here: it is nine o'clock, right? Well, if I told you what has happened while I was 'making time' in order to come and rob you of yours, you surely would change your opinion.

"Well sir, as soon as night began to fall and the trees of the Prado were attracting a pernicious dew, it occurred to me that I could do nothing better than refresh my gullet which had become dry with the dust and movement of my long walk. The nearby Solís saloon seemed to offer relief, but there were so many who had calculated just as I that I couldn't even get a seat; actually, I wasn't too sorry because this gave me the opportunity to go enjoy an exquisite pink punch at Amato's place, the famous confectioner. Just imagine how sweet it is to drink a pink punch in a gorgeous room; to see pass before you the elegant concurrence of ladies and gentlemen who, descending from shining carriages, arrive to render the tribute of their admiration to that kindly host! Unfortunately, this operation cannot be prolonged more than fifteen minutes. *Sic transit gloria mundi!* At the end of this brief spell, what else can one do but take leave of that elegant locale, and search elsewhere for new sensations?

"Politics! What an immense field for an observer! Luckily, the Nuevo café suddenly pops up. Noisy den! Confusion! What news I found about there! What wordy speeches I heard! What plans for ending the war! How I dissertated and argued! I resembled Bernadote himself! But my head ached, and there was nothing to do but take the steps of Levante; what I mean is, I climbed the stairway of the café of that name. Transition, romantic contrast, 1835 and 1805.

"To ease a headache there is nothing like sitting down to a game of chess with a scribe; but the circle of onlookers which pressed in around us was enough to cut off our air supply. The cigarette smoke, the odor of the coffee (which, by the way, is excellent), the monotonous noise of the pawns and queens, of the balls and cues, of the dice and domino pieces ..., let the game wait for another day; let's move on to the billiard hall; now there is a peaceful room! An immovable circle around the table, a silent council of grave men, an original scene illuminated from directly above worthy of the brush of Teniers. And why all of this? To observe the movements of two round balls pushed along even rounder paths. *Oh raras hominum mentes!*

"The nearby cafés of Lorencini and the Fontana were too *classical* for me, composed of elderly rich folk who discussed at length the cholera outbreak of last year or the straw and utensil tax of this year; but what formality...! Give me laughter and noise and...look, there is no better café than the Príncipe in the world: there is plenty to see and hear in the Príncipe. Do you enjoy politics? All the latest news turns up in this Madrilenian Lloyd. Do you have a turn for political law? Just listen to a hundred lawyers. Diplomacy? Ancient and modern to pick from. Morality? Many adventures are known about there. Poetry? The modern Parnasillo is situated there. Journalists? The fountain of all wisdom itself. Romanticism? It is just like Venice! Material pleasures, drinks? A half a shot for two *reales*. A rigid, severe atmosphere? Go across the street or to Morenillo's billiard parlor.

"Anything can be fatiguing, nevertheless, and I was now as tired as can be from all the clamor; but time was standing still, and it was only eight o'clock according to the boisterous announcement barked forth by the playing of the military retreat, the sound of which proceeded forth in various directions from the Puerta del Sol, and was accompanied by a group of disheveled Andromaches that were marching to the rhythm of the war drums.

"Fleeing, as is natural, from all that noise that was aimed down Alcalá Street toward the military quarters, I suddenly stopped on Peligros Street, and there, where the advocate for all that is lost is displayed for public veneration in a famous painting, I paused to reflect upon my direction. Oh, Mr. Curious Chatterbox, how I would like to have your brush to outline for you the shady scenes that I witnessed! Believe me, very few turns of a country dance or of the mazurka come out so practiced as those that were formed before my eyes by the fetching neighborhood girls with their round, full figures, and by the clever fanciers of flirtations, both groups alternately appearing and disappearing through the intersections of Hita, Gitanos, Peligros, San Jerónimo, Príncipe, and Cruz Streets; but since the 'darkness of the night and the roughness of the terrain allowed them to hide their movements from me,' and since, on the other hand, I remember that you have already described these doings for us

in your ballad *Jane's Stroll*, I will add nothing more, nor will I
insist on following step by step the sensitive couples that freely
entered a wine shop, the latter with very few locks or bolts,
thanks to the foresightful perceptiveness of the owner; nor
the music-loving street walkers, who, standing on a corner in
front of a singing blind man, spin their cobweb like a spider,
not without the appreciation of a large group of muffled dead-
beats; nor, in short, the women who, as they entered into the
noisy taverns with their mantillas slung over their heads, greatly
rejuvenated the spirit of those bacchanal gatherings. This scene
alone, which I witnessed standing on Toledo Street, deserves
a separate article, and I promise to give you the whole story."

"Can I get a word in?"

"And after all that I've said, would you term this way of
'making time' a waste? No, but now come around praising all
these clubs and societies, those foreign academies and lyceums.
Would you want, for example, our writers and other interested
parties to have private gatherings where they could meet during
these hours and discuss their works? Would you propose that
common men find inexpensive shows to which they could go
so as to witness the skills of an athlete or the nonsense of a
buffoon? Would you desire that the libraries be open at such an
hour, and that it were proper for both sexes to appear there?
Would you praise, in short, the intimate evening gatherings
with their games of forfeit and their platonic love affairs? Drat
them all! Anyway, where can you find them now?

"If you don't think so, just go up to the house of your friend
Melquíades Revesino. The door is closed . . . , wonder if it is
two knocks or three . . . , let's try two.

" 'Who is it?' asks an indignant old lady from the third floor.

" 'A man.'

" 'What room do you want?'

" 'Number two.'

"And she closes the balcony, and you are stuck in the street.

"Let's say that out of charity she opens the door; let's say that
you ring the bell for room two, and that the women of the house
are not home, and that the only response you receive is the
barking of the pet dog, and that, in short, there is no one
home . . . My goodness, it certainly is a wonderful experience to

be alone in a dark stairway with the front entrance locked!

"But get up the nerve and slip out of this spot by the recourse of appeal, or whatever, at the home of the lawyer Sir Pánfilo. Look at the whole family, taken aback by your unannounced visit; they are asking you: 'What is this, Mr. So and So? You in these parts? What brings about all this? Is there something going on? Has something happened?'

" 'No, my friends; only the wish to see you all.'

" 'My gosh, it is not possible; Margarita, put that sewing away, come over here; and you, Toribio, advise the man of the house, he is in the den.'

" 'No, don't bother him.'

" 'Take away that oil lamp, and bring some candles.'

" 'Please, don't go to any trouble.'

"In short, you observe (and it is not hard to perceive) that you have ruffled the waters of tranquility, and in order to bail yourself out, in order to 'make time,' you have to improvise what is almost a declaration of love to one of the daughters.

"But what is this? Are you writing hieroglyphs while I speak? Are you 'making time' also?"

"Not at all; I am composing my article, or, to put it more properly, you are composing it for me since I am merely taking down in shorthand what you are recounting."

"Really? And what has come of all of this?"

"It has turned out just as I wanted: a sketch of Madrid during the early evening that will make another one even better."

"What's that?"

"Yes, my friend; I had outlined the background; you have given it real vitality."

II *The Analysis*

In the Early Evening is similar to the majority of sketches by Mesonero; in these the author skillfully combines humor and entertainment value with criticism of contemporary mores. Both aspects come forth in various ways, the humor principally serving to mask, without completely hiding, a clearly definable set of values which the author is attempting to communicate. The necessity in mass publications of preaching without seeming to preach was clearly understood by Mesonero.

The sketch begins with a declaration of the main theme: the extravagance or extreme wastefulness of Spaniards with all things, especially time. Mesonero promotes his theme by employing long, complex sentences with frequent listlike accumulations of examples. The ironic humor in this verbosity is apparent as is the successful establishment of an emotional rapport with the reader: the latter sees the writer as being "one of us." The critical posture the narrator assumes before his theme is more intellectual than emotional as can be seen in this example and throughout his article.

On another plane these "distances" can also be considered primarily temporal as opposed to spatial. Mesonero seems partially out of touch with his times. His sympathetic references to the past, and his denigrating contrasts of this past with the present promote this vision. Spatially, however, the author is all Spaniard, not at all removed from his people or his place. Even though his defense of lyceums, academies, libraries, and the work ethic seem to align him intellectually with the progressive thought of some northern Europeans, the humor, the self-deprecating irony, and other stylistic considerations make it clear that Mesonero saw the charm and the color of the Spanish way. This is the same dichotomy that Larra expressed in many of his articles. However, for "Fígaro" the split was serious, even tragic; he could never reconcile himself to it. For Mesonero, the disharmony was also serious, but he managed to keep his sense of humor and accept inner conflict as inevitable, as part of life.

Pursuant to the humor in the sketch, we have already mentioned the ironic verbosity and mazelike lengthy sentences which at times make it difficult to trace the antecedent. Another principal source of humor is the element of surprising reversals. These reversals are both verbal and dramatic. An example of the former occurs in the first paragraph when Mesonero declares that generosity is a distinguishing trait of the Spaniard. In the following sentences, the idea of generosity quickly comes to mean wastefulness or extravagance. Dramatic reversals appear with frequency, especially within the prolonged series of questions and answers that begins in the fourth paragraph. A street loafer becomes an amorous consort for a businessman's wife, and the same businessman becomes a loafer. A pensive-looking judge becomes a lazy, hungry man, precisely as does a statuelike construction worker. The humor is a function of the unexpected twist of the original statement; again we may note the plethora of examples, the stylistic *extravagance.*

Exaggeration is one of Mesonero's most frequent tactics for stimulating humor, and it is abundantly employed in this sketch. Overstatement is facile humor; it can be counted upon to promote the narrator-reader identification Mesonero seeks as well as to simply entertain. Those who have viewed this aspect of Mesonero's art with disfavor, such as Berkowitz,[3] have themselves exaggerated, stating that Don Ramón stoops to the level of a comic strip, or that he distorts reality to such a degree that all realism is lost. In any case, Mesonero overdraws in order to provoke laughter and to reduce his arguments to simpler terms. For example, in the first paragraph he extravagantly states that all the extravagant statements made in one day in Spain, if gathered, could serve as a "... guidebook of proclamations for every country of the globe." One suspects also that he overstates the contrast between the ancestors' ways and the modern habits as regards the use of leisure time. Hyperbole is most obviously present in the accumulation of colorful incidents that befall Don Pascual during his early evening stroll.

The narrative dialogue of Don Pascual in the second half of the article is replete with comic situations. To single out only one, we may point to the concluding lines in which first the door is slammed in Pascual's face, then he is left stranded in a dark hallway, and finally he is a rather unwilling guest of some less-than-close friends who were not expecting him. The embarrassment and tension for both parties is a sure stimulus for laughter. To extract himself from the situation, Don Pascual must hastily improvise a declaration of love to one of the daughters.

The final major source of humor may be termed verbal. The narrator's ironic and seemingly unconscious stylistic revelation of the same flaws as those he criticizes has already been noted. Don Pascual also expresses himself humorously; his selection of words reveals an attitude that favors pleasures of the superficially elite. He does, however, have the capacity for surprising, expressive juxtapositions such as when he contrasts Amato's place with the Nuevo Café by calling them a "... romantic contrast, 1835 and 1805."

The irony Don Pascual focuses upon himself as he recounts the evening's activities is similar although more obvious and meaningful than that of the narrator. This irony is meant to function both to create humor and to forward the theme. The basis is Don Pascual's coincidental assertion that the new methods of utilizing leisure time are more fulfilling than those of the past while he demonstrates that they are not. Through his narrative and his manner of speech, he demonstrates the shallowness, the immorality, and the utter confusion of contemporary social life. He even admits that this chaos was fatiguing, unhealthy, and monotonous. He arrives at the narrator's house unfulfilled and with a headache.

If one scrutinizes the structure of these paragraphs, he will generally note several opening lines of affirmation followed by an unintentional description of the superficiality, the monotony, the confusion, or the immorality of these activities. Don Pascual's examples prove precisely the opposite of his intention. The irony again reaches the deepest aspects of style: syntax and vocabulary. Nearly every paragraph begins with a fully structured sentence and soon dissolves into fragmentation. The sentence construction parallels the chaotic activities described. Don Pascual seems blithely unaware that his pseudolearned Latin phrases and other words such as "noisy," "confusion," "headache," "monotonous," "fatiguing," and "shady scenes" impart more criticism than praise upon his scene.

The final irony appears at the conclusion when Pascual proposes to show the narrator that the old time pleasures are nonexistent even if desirable. For his example he chooses the home of Don Melquíades Revesino. However Don Pascual cancels the utility of his presentation by causing the Revesino family to be out, and by unexpectedly dropping in on some near strangers. His example proves nothing; the ironical humor cannot be missed. His sarcastically expressed list of alternatives to contemporary pleasures—academies, libraries, literary societies, intimate social gatherings—are then obviously superior to the confusion he has described. Don Pascual has unconsciously destroyed his own argument, providing support for the narrator's thesis in a very entertaining fashion. As Mesonero concludes the sketch, "I had outlined the background; you have given it real vitality."

Beyond its entertainment value, humor is employed for a strategic approximation of the reader to the narrator. Once this empathy is established, the writer is more likely to gain acceptance for his point of view. The mild self-deprecating irony of the narrator at the outset also serves this same purpose. Further devices are employed. The rather racy description of night life in the popular district is sure to be enjoyed by most readers as are the few verses sung by the construction worker. More important than this, however, is Mesonero's inclusion of references to himself as a writer, to his process of composition of this same article, and to three of his previous articles. All of these techniques reestablish the familiarity of the readers of Madrid with the "Curious Chatterbox" and his *costumbrista* world. The reader seems to be on the inside, seeing the very article take shape. Familiarity is also increased in that Mesonero continues his construction of a coherent fictive world much like that of the Galdosian novel by repeatedly employing the same familiar characters in his sketches. Don Melquíades Revesino is a principal actor in two sketches previous to this one as is Don Pascual Bailón Corredera. The reader's familiarity with these names and these articles certainly acts as a magnet, drawing him closer to the narrator. Also significant is a heightened sense of realism in the sketches; if "fictive" characters can appear and converse with the author during the process of composition, then the articles themselves take on an added aura of documentation based upon real life.

If one studies the character of Don Pascual in his previous appearances, his view of this actor as an agent of irony is increased. Pascual is a hyperactive, man about town who always seems to know everyone, but never seems to avoid problems, even real trouble. In *Los cómicos en Cuaresma* (*The Actors at Lent*) he becomes involved in amorous intrigues among some actresses, and in *La capa vieja y el baile de candil* (*The Old Cape and the Spirited Dance Party*) we read an account of his youthful escapades which concluded with his confinement in jail.

In any case, both the humor and the folly of this familiar character clearly serve Mesonero's purposes in this sketch.

The humor and the gentle ironies of this sketch have been signalled above, but it is also true that some moralization or serious criticism is present. One notes, however, a preponderance of a familiar or light tone. The alert narrator cunningly buries his preaching in the center portion of the sketch, after the confidence of the reader has been gained. The paragraphs following the humorous question-answer portion are given to serious criticism. The writer rails against the siesta, the long evening strolls, the idle visits paid to friends, and the politically oriented, foul-smelling cafés which no longer resemble the decorous soda fountains of the past. The most significant vehicle for Don Ramón's criticism is the value-charged word—especially the adjective—which he employs generously. Such words as "apathetic," "unwisely," "aimlessly," "fictitious," "pleasurable," "lovable," and "true" leave little doubt as to the writer's sense of priorities. After only three paragraphs of this, Mesonero again turns to criticism through gentle irony as he ushers in Don Pascual. One senses that the direct comments just prior to Pascual's humorous scene principally serve to condition the reader, causing the latter to see Don Pascual in the "proper" light. This is precisely the same movement from the general to the specific that is almost always a characteristic of Mesonero's articles. The general portion, regardless of its basic content, is normally a vehicle for at least some moral or ethical orientation for the reader. The characters with their humorous mini-scenes enter later to provide concrete exemplification for the previous statements.

Another aspect of this sketch which is typical of many is the varied approach to the presentation of the material. The emphasis is on change, on miniunits, on thematic unity with compositional diversity. The article begins as would an essay, with a general discussion of a broad topic. In a first movement toward specificity, the writer conjures up five small scenes, each with its own cast of characters, even including some song in verse for further variety. As noted above, the next four paragraphs resemble an essay, even a sermon. The second half of the article is principally a narrative dialogue in which temporal unity is maintained, but great spatial and human variety is present. Variety, movement, and vitality are all typically present in Don Ramón's *cuadros*. As is usual, however, the fast-moving parade of characters precludes any possibility of penetrating their inner world. A sketch by Mesonero can only dramatize flashes of behavior; rarely can it even aspire to suggest emotions, conflicts, or motivations. The intention is to suggest typicalness by the force of accumulation. The author can, however, treat deeper human dimensions in his essaylike general remarks at the beginning or the conclusion of his articles.

In a broad sense, then, *In the Early Evening* aspires to paint a portrait of the deterioration across several generations of characteristic leisure time activities. As suggested above, however, the sketch is not free of a certain ambivalence. While Mesonero intellectually deplores the wasted time, the relaxed morals, and the new attraction of the plebeian districts and customs, he does not deny that the Spanish way still preserves a certain magic. The following phrase most succinctly captures this ambivalence (italics mine): "But in the midst of our lavishness, with nothing are we more extravagant than with our time, and there is nothing, in truth, that we know how to waste with more *charm* and *fortitude*." This playful treatment of his theme, a technique which dominates these pages, goes far to communicate a vision of a concerned but resigned—even coyly smiling—author. The writer does not hold himself morally superior to his reader, at least not to any significant degree. The irony touches everyone, and is gentle in all cases. Above all, the reader seems to gain a friend as he amusedly reads of his own weaknesses and vices.

III *Classifications*

Any attempt to rigidly classify the *costumbrista* sketches ultimately proves unsatisfactory because of their great number, the multiple purposes of many, and the extraordinary flexibility of the genre itself. Especially when grouped by theme or ideological intention, Mesonero's writings seem ineluctably elusive. Various critics, especially in manuals of literary history, have copied Ferrer del Río's division which points to articles that describe Spain's old order, those that depict the new customs, and those that show the transition.[4] Two difficulties are present with this scheme. First, the author rarely devotes exclusive attention to any one of these themes: usually they are combined as in *1802 y 1832* (*1802 and 1832*) or *Antes, ahora y después* (*Then, Now and Later*). Also, after treating these three types of articles, one is left with many which do not fit. The critic must be satisfied with incompleteness, or continue his classification in a new direction such as by genre, tone, or technique. Pitollet and his later imitators provide examples of this confusion. It seems most advisable to recognize as integral to the definition of the genre a noticeable elasticity in subject matter, theme, technique, and style. Each sketch, in a limited way, creates its own rules similar to the novel.

Potentially, the material could be divided into three sub-genres: (1) the scene, (2) the essay, and (3) the human type. The first category refers to a description of a place, a custom, or an institution in which some narrative or dramatic element enlivens and unifies the material. This is the most abundant grouping, one in which Mesonero usually found most success. At times, such as in *De tejas arriba* (*From the Roof Up*) or *El día de toros* (*Bullfight Day*), these sketches resemble the short story. The term "essay" is used here in a special, private sense; it refers to those articles with a more discursive style, those in which the intellectual or purely critical or scholarly intention predominates. The third group, human types, alludes to a form more pursued by Mesonero in the 1840s and thereafter, coincidentally with the new vogue of the French inspired *fisiología* ("physiology"). *Los españoles pintados por sí mismos* (*The Spaniards in a Self-Portrait*), 1843–1844, best represents this new enthusiasm for the typical man rather than the typical scene.

However, the constant overlapping and blending of genre, tone, technique, and intention creates weaknesses with any rigid scheme. For this reason, I will hold to loose principles of organization, treating themes and techniques which seem paramount. This will allow discussion of certain hybrid sketches within several categories.

IV   *The Flat Character Type*

Mesonero Romanos, as did the majority of *costumbristas*, realized that the one dimensional or "flat" character best suited his purposes and the limited space available in the periodical press.[5] This kind of character is easily subordinated to a larger entity, the scene, the true expressive intent of most *costumbristas*. In terms of literary evolution, Mesonero gradually turned more and more to the sketch devoted solely to the character type. This culminated in 1861 with his last *costumbrista* work called *Types, Groups, and Outlines of Costumbrista Sketches*. Don Ramón's most successful articles, however, are those earlier ones in which he drew one or more human figures, and established their relationship within a larger narrative framework.

Of the vast human cast which populates these sketches, the majority belong to a category that may be defined as background characters. These are mostly faceless folk, glimpsed during their characteristic leisure time activities such as the afternoon stroll and the evening *tertulia*. Frequently the author allows the spotlight to focus momentarily on one or several of these persons. They come to the forefront and their dialogue is overheard—at times without identification of the speaker—or their representative actions are portrayed. When this happens they correspond to what Henry James has called the "ficelle," that is, the character who belongs not to the subject but to the treatment. Used as an expressive tool to serve the larger entity—the scene—these characters disappear as soon as they have exercised their function. They are the beginnings of types, flattened by their anonymity, the brevity of their appearance, and their clear relation to the scene's governing idea. Mesonero often negates any possible individuality in these characters by describing their typical activities in the impersonal plural form.

More important characters are also frequently depersonalized, and made to function as moral or social illustrations. This is accomplished by many means. The most direct method is Mesonero's blunt admission within the sketches that he only seeks to depict social or moral tendencies. He insists that his characters are not patterned after specific individuals: they are only embodiments of vices and other traits. These comments condition the reader's attitude, predisposing him to ignore any indi-

viduality and to search for these characters' obvious symbolical
value. Don Ramón affirms that "...the characters that of course
I will describe are not portraits, but sketches of types or figures,
just as I do not pretend to be a portrait-painter, but only a
painter" (II, p. 11). Again he states, "...nor gaily repeat those
idealistic types which enabled us to develop and realize that
idea" (II, p. 286). In another essay, in the midst of a description,
the author generalizes his human figures by exclaiming: "But
slow down there, talking pen; we should not desert the type
which concerns us today" (II, p 234).

In a related manner, Mesonero often directly or indirectly
announces the essence to which his type will correspond, and
then fills the mold with particularizing characteristics. Even
the most memorable characters such as Mauricio R. of *El amante
corto de vista* (*The Nearsighted Lover*) normally do not escape
the introductory generalizations. However, at times the detail
is so vivid and the manner of presentation so striking that the
type comes alive. This intensifies the author's message. At the
beginning of *El día 30 del mes* (*The 30th of the Month*), one
reads: "Satisfaction and joy seem to have chosen for their
mansion that face which time in vain attempts to wrinkle"
(I, p. 99). The remainder of the study is a vision of this governing idea in human form as it relates to the characteristic
activities of the government's payday.

A step toward subtlety is often taken by means of certain
structural arrangements. The author may begin on a timeless,
generalized note. An introductory philosophical, historical, moralistic, or esthetic discussion is typically followed by a wide-
angle description of the particular problem in Spanish society,
and, in step three, is finally reduced to exemplification through
manipulated types and situations. This tripartite structure with
its ever-narrowing focus is often completed with a return to the
general view by means of a moral statement or summarylike
conclusion. The fictive characters are esthetically distanced from
the reader, structurally embedded in a larger whole—a sort of
Chinese box; their functionality and subordination are easy to
perceive. Also, the writer has little space in which to individu-
alize his creations since they do not appear until the midportion
of the sketch. In *Pretender por alto* (*To Start at the Top*), for

example, Mesonero begins with several paragraphs of observations regarding social and economic realities in Madrid. He then narrows the focus as he describes typical scenes found by those who seek a place in the overstocked bureaucracy; the sketch is finally brought to the level of concrete experience by means of a tale which illustrates the evils in the system. A short sermonette concludes the article, thus effectively distancing the reader, negating any approximations he may have made to the characters as people. At the conclusion the latter are removed from the field of action and feeling. They are returned to philosophy and ethics.

Three other partly external factors also promote generality and explicit character definition. The titles, for example, usually announce a broad social theme, thus suggesting a narrow role for the individual literary figure. Such titles as *La empleomanía* (*A Mania for Government Employment*), *Las tiendas* (*The Shops*), and *La posada, o España en Madrid* (*The Boarding-house, or Spain in Madrid*) may serve as examples. In a comparable manner, most sketches commence with an epigraph often taken from traditional native literary sources or a wide variety of foreign writers, mostly French. These pronouncements summarize some aspect of the content, surrounding the characters and action with an aura of timelessness and definition. The human figures lose their potential for spontaneity and surprise in such an atmosphere. In the same *The 30th of the Month* we read: "Reversals of fortune/misery is called by some:/why, if these reversals/obviously owe to witless conduct?" (I, p. 99). This dictum of Samaniego then hangs over Don Homo-bono Quiñones, predetermining the reader's vision and possibly the author's creative possibilities. Mesonero's notes (written for the fifth edition of 1851) represent a third extrinsic technique of definition. While many of these deal with circumstances of authorship, publication, and social change, many also inject authorial interpretation upon the scenes and the types. In a concluding note to *The 30th of the Month*, Mesonero defines Don Homo-bono as a "... type based upon the employee of the old days, trustworthy, industrious, and routine-loving" (I, p. 101).

Names are usually treated in one of three ways, each one of which further contributes to easy identification without the complications of individual personality. Certain heavy-handed symbolical labels combine humor (or entertainment value) and definition. The principal recurring figures receive names which vivify the author's thesis. A fellow skilled at swindling newcomers to Madrid is called Don Solícito Ganzúa (he who "solicits" by "picking locks"); a happy, rather thoughtless man is labelled Don Plácido Cascabellilo (a "placid" rattle-brained fellow); a father who never seems to properly deal with his children, always needing moralistic advice from the narrator, is Don Melquíades Revesino (the high priest of backwardness); and, finally, a jovial man about town who enjoys night life and seems to know everyone is Don Pascual Bailón Corredera (the dancing high-stepper). In a similar fashion, the frequent employment of labels such as *galán* ("courtier" or "well-made man"), *orador* ("orator"), and *ninfa* ("young lady") clearly aids in typing the characters. Mesonero also leaves certain persons nameless, especially those of the nobility such as the marquis in *Grandeza y miseria* (*Grandeur and Misery*). This may well be attributable to social timidity or fear of reprisal. Time and space, it might be added, are treated in a parallel manner. Very infrequently does one find precision as to when or where the events occur, especially in those articles critical of some aspect of Spanish life. Even street names are avoided; instead, the author employs ellipsis dots. Through carefully cultivated techniques promoting generality and vagueness, Mesonero sought a wider social or moral application of his thesis than would be possible if he drew particularized, complex human figures or if he carefully delimited time and space.

Human individuality is also lessened by the intimate relationship which Mesonero often establishes between tangible objects and literary personages. Matrimonial fidelity is stamped upon one character by his devotion to a cot which has been associated with that trait for generations; frivolity is attached to those who spend their days consumed by the problems involved in obtaining theater tickets, new clothing, or a horse-drawn carriage. A most memorable example is found in *The Old Cape and the Spirited Dance Party* when Don Pascual Bailón Corredera sees a portion of his youth and some of his earlier attitudes summed up in an old cape which he once wore. In *El sombrerito y la mantilla* (*The Little Hat and the Shawl*) such vague but sweeping traits as Spanish traditionalism and French-inspired innovation are linked to two girls who are identified with the time-honored Spanish shawl (Paquita), and the modern, elegant, foreign-inspired hats (Serafina). This subordination of human figures to objects is, then, another method of achieving simplification and definition—two basic purposes of the *costumbrista*.

For many reasons, including its association with the periodical press and with a mass readership, the *costumbrista* article may be considered a relatively pedestrian or prosaic literary form. In spite of this, Mesonero does incorporate imaginative elements which, although they do not suggest great creativity, do provide variety and also function to lessen the particularity of the characterizations. In *El Prado* (*The Prado*) the author announces that the scene and the characters have not been observed but imagined or re-created: "Let's pretend that we see him on a tranquil summer afternoon...." (I, p. 77). Examples comparable to this abound in the *Scenes of Madrid*.

Several variations on this explicit denial of character realism exist. In *From the Roof Up,* one of Mesonero's most vigorous approximations to particularity and the short story, the author apparently sensed he had, in Doña Claudia, created a rather unique, free-standing character. After a particularly expressive dialogue, he disassembles the characterization by partially denying what he had just written: "I do not know if the old woman spoke precisely in these or other terms, nor am I able to ascertain if she was really this talented with respect to the comparisons which give strength and persuasiveness to her discourse..." (II, p. 132). Another version of the same technique is the rapid, even shocking undoing of the creation at the conclusion of an article. After graphically describing an enjoyable party, an encounter with a girl friend out of his past, even the more youthful attitude which suddenly possessed him, the author concludes *El Salón de Oriente* (*The East Club*) with the following revelation: "The illusion disappeared. Everything can be explained. The hall was my bedroom; the one that paged me was my Galician servant; the dance was a dream; and my kind couple, ethereal, bodyless, impalpable..., it was, in short, my imagination, that still does not want to give up its youth" (II, p. 27). A final variation is exemplified in *La almoneda* (*The Auction*). After individualizing Don Policarpo de la Transfiguración Omnibus de los Santos—a multifaceted, energetic character—Mesonero abruptly divests his creation of flesh, treating him in imaginative, almost mythic terms. Don Policarpo is shown to be omnipresent, and is compared to a ghostly apparition: "And this is so certain, that some days past, having climbed to the tower of Santa Cruz, it seemed to me that I was seeing him at the same time in Montera Street and in the Prado, in the Plaza de Oriente and in the Canal, and in the Toledo Entrance, and right there in the tower with me; he followed me and persecuted me like a fantastic, inevitable, impassible apparition, similar to a stubborn nightmare or the endless, monotonous noise of a waterfall" (II, pp. 78–79).

All of these examples demonstrate, then, various means by which Mesonero effectively minimized any connections between his characters and individual human life. Many other devices remain, but will be treated more briefly. For example, Mesonero often categorizes his characters by letting them speak with heavy rustic or regional dialects. This method is particularly successful in *The Boardinghouse, or Spain in Madrid,* an article in which Don Ramón sketches a series of types systematically selected to represent each corner of provincial Spain. Speech is employed for geographical typing, and thought patterns, possessions, and dress demonstrate age and occupation. The weight of meaning oppressively hangs over this static list of characters until they are brought together to interact in the final portion.

At other moments, Mesonero generalizes his figures by comparing them to characters from classical mythology, the Bible, or other literature as well as with timeless proverbs and diverse art objects. In one paragraph, Doña Dorotea Ventosa is variously likened to a beautifully covered ancient book of laws, a certain restored classical painting, and a well-conserved battle helmet from ancient Greek society which had been restored so often that ". . . it was always the same, although it had completely disappeared" (II, p. 104). Toward the same end, he also converts his characters into models of traditional Spanish or contemporary foreign social behavior patterns. The latter is demonstrated at length by means of the son of Don Melquíades Revesino in *El extranjero en su patria* (*The Stranger in His Own Country*). This boy, educated during his youth in France, absorbs that country's tastes and values to the extent that he later rejects Spanish life styles when he returns to his native country as a young man. In all cases, these characters are subordinated to something larger than themselves, made to "stand for" rather than simply "be."

Aiding significantly in the reader's perception of Don Ramón's creations as one dimensional characters is the fact that the author often employs the basic universal comedy types in easily recognizable situations. Whether we utilize Northrup Frye's system of the two opposed pairs,[6] or whether we simply follow more traditional schemes of stock comedy types, it is not difficult to recognize these patterns and to note the reappearance of many in several essays, thus promoting even more facile identification. The conspiring servants of *Grandeur and Misery* fit the pattern of the *dolosus servus* or tricky slave; Don Melquíades Revesino, who attempts to protect his daughter Jacinta from a bad marriage in *Los aires del lugar* (*Country Breezes*) is the *senex iratus* or angry father; Doña Dorotea Ventosa, in *Las tres tertulias* (*The Three Evening Social Gatherings*), strongly suggests the imposter pattern by her empty pretentiousness; and Juan Algarrobo of *El recién venido* (*The Newcomer*) is the perfect gull, the innocent, easily cheated type. Examples of the fop or conceited dandy abound: one finds them conversing in the walkways and plazas of numerous sketches by Mesonero.

Don Ramón is not content, however, to simply place universal types within a Spanish context; often our author develops prototypes of special characters normally more identified with Spain alone. Often they are related to the specific tensions and realities of the mid-nineteenth century. The materialistic young widow already being courted before the burial of her rich husband is seen in several articles, as is the ignorant fellow who has developed a fanaticism for a certain activity, such as politics, but whose conversation is entirely made up of phrases taken from the morning newspaper. A more serious recurring type who is dramatized in various forms is the pathetically tragic figure living according to the outdated values of the past in a rapidly changing cosmopolitan society. Don Perpetuo Antañón in *La casa a la antigua* (*The House from Times Past*) attempts to isolate and protect his young daughter according to the traditional Spanish manner; the results, of course, are tragic. The daughter is forced to break free from this repression; she does so in a relatively direct manner according to the changing attitudes of the times.

Normally, when Mesonero brings back his previously treated types, they evince precisely the same characteristics in each article. Several exceptions exist: in these instances one may speak of slightly rounded personalities and a clear increase in individual human interest. In *La comedia casera* (*A Stage Play at Home*), an article which may be classified as slapstick burlesque, and also in *The Three Evening Social Gatherings*, Don Plácido Cascabellilo is a happy-go-lucky personality. His name seems ironic, however, in the article *1802 and 1832*, since both he and the narrator lament the worsening moral character of the modern youth. The most striking example of change involves Juan Algarrobo. In *The Newcomer* he plays the naive country cousin, robbed and mistreated by everyone during his first days in Madrid. Time passes, experience is gained, and in *The Boardinghouse, or Spain in Madrid* Juan suddenly displays the same aggressive deviousness that had victimized him earlier. Previously defeated, he turns out the victor in a new contest of wit and nerve.

It is true that Don Ramón prefers to exercise ideological control over his character types, but he does allow them great freedom of action and speech. By the latter I mean that the author prefers indirect methods of characterization rather than direct. Instead of static blocks of exposition, description, analysis, or direct statements of definition by other characters within the sketches, Don Ramón, once he reaches the moment of specificity, normally allows his creations to portray their own significance through their speech, actions, and interaction with their environment and with other characters. This type of characterization partly accounts for the vivacity that Mesonero's types demonstrate in relatively few paragraphs. Don Ramón's realism is not of detail, process, or complexity, but of intensity, singleness, and quick illumination. Don Plácido Cascabellilo appears in three articles, but is never described by the narrator. Always made to speak and act, this character and most others grow out of situation as well as the introductory ideological framework. Through dynamic techniques of characterization, Mesonero at once achieves simple, one dimensional personages who can carry a message and yet be vividly seen in the reader's imagination.

V *Other Details of Composition*

Most of the above comments on style, structure, and technique treat typical, recurring aspects of Mesonero's writings. It is important now to succinctly refer to several other traits so as to draw a more complete portrait of his imaginative prose.

One useful organizing principle for any discussion of Mesonero's style and techniques is variety. I have already alluded to numerous manifestations of this factor. Although variety promotes interest and is a useful guard against reader boredom, it also effectively prevents profound examination of particular themes. Any sense of depth within Mesonero's sketches is attained by dint of accumulation. The resultant impression is one of rapidity, of restlessness, of movement, and of a shifting narrative or descriptive perspective which primarily skims over the surface of people, objects, and ideas.

There are many means by which Mesonero obtains variety. One of the most visible is the form in which he organizes the presentation. In fact, it is not uncommon for Mesonero to discuss this topic with the reader at the beginning of the sketch. As seen above, this heightened reader-narrator intimacy serves the ultimate didactic intention. Some of Don Ramón's articles are ostensibly based on an interview or a conversation of the writer with a friend after the former has found himself without literary inspiration. This was seen to some extent in *In the Early Evening*. Mesonero may conveniently receive a visit from a colorful character, he may seek out a conversation with an old friend or neighbor, or he may simply proceed to the streets in search of local color. This stroll technique—either with or without a friend with whom he may converse—is undoubtedly the most characteristic organizing principle of his sketches.

Other articles, such as *To Start at the Top*, are based upon

the activities of Don Ramón in behalf of relatives or friends
from distant cities who have business in Madrid. Several times
the author even publishes letters which he has supposedly
received from readers in the capital or in the provinces. In other
cases, Mesonero begins on a direct note of action or incident:
in *El día de fiesta* (*The Day of a Party*), the form is free, un-
directed dialogue; in *Bullfight Day*, it is descriptive-narrative.
Also, not infrequently, the author commences with certain historical, descriptive, or moral considerations. The tendency
toward a more static, essaylike beginning increases as the *Scenes
of Madrid* progress.

Don Ramón has demonstrated himself the master of various
tones. Hartzenbusch refers to a wide gamut of possible reader
reactions which he relates to the tone of the sketches: (1) a
malicious smile in *El paseo de Juana* (*Jane's Stroll*); (2) a
boisterous laugh in *The Newcomer;* (3) a state of melancholy
in *A Mania for Government Employment;* (4) a heartfelt emotion
in *Una noche de vela* (*A Night at Vigil*); and (5) a startling
jolt in *El camposanto* (*The Cemetery*). The same critic, taking
issue with others who refer to Mesonero's prose as always pale,
concludes: "Now that is knowing how to write: to know how to
feel, to know how to think."[7] I conclude that these descriptions
of Hartzenbusch are suggestive, but partially exaggerated.
Mesonero's many techniques promoting vagueness and generality
plus the constant moral distance between himself and the material
tend to diminish the emotional immediacy of his prose. At the
time he composed *The Picture*, Don Ramón was merely twenty-
nine years of age; his moral severity, however, manifests the
mentality of an elderly observer from the previous era. Even the
sketches that can be considered festive are usually more subdued
than, for example, a *sainete* of Ramón de la Cruz.

Other aspects of variety aid in the creation of this sense of
vitality. Allusion has previously been made to a shifting narrative
or descriptive perspective. This mobile point of view is partially
a function of the stroll technique. Mesonero is frequently in the
streets reporting on small scenes as they occur in the plazas,
streets, and shops, as well as during pilgrimages, holiday gatherings, and other special occasions. Another key element is the
second voice of the sketch, usually a friend, relative, or neighbor

with whom the author converses. By this means a double perspective is established toward the action or the theme. As seen above, Don Ramón takes care to establish the proper moral relationships so that the reader will perceive the flaws (if existent) in one point of view and the correctness in the other. These minor clashes explain the frequency with which the reader finds expressions of surprise, shock, and disagreement; these often take the form of startled exclamations and ironic questions. Added perspective is gained when the conversation is between Don Ramón and a foreigner, a man from the provinces, or a native of Madrid who has long been absent. Temporal perspective is also present in various ways; at times Don Ramón and a friend discuss the younger generation (usually the problems of the friend's children), and at other moments the writer directly contrasts new customs with old (*The Little Hat and the Shawl*). As the *Scenes of Madrid* progress, it becomes more common for "The Curious Chatterbox" to recede into the background, taking the part of the listener rather than that of the more aggressive commentator.

A sense of vitality is also promoted by the wide variety of characters that populate these sketches. Even though some reappear frequently, the total number is impressive. Many social classes, with their logically differing forms of diction (linguistic variety), are also present. Socially, Mesonero's articles extend from the lofty levels of nobility to the lower levels of criminality. A sense of a full human presence with voices buzzing in the background exists. Frequently the author—without introduction—includes relatively short bursts of anonymous dialogue in order to convey the sense of outdoor reality. Adding to this sense of fullness, Don Ramón rarely treats his characters as they labor. He prefers a view of man at leisure—usually public leisure—or involved in some activity divorced from economic pursuits. Apparently the author felt that these moments more fully revealed the nature of the people; leisure time is also, of course, more colorful and more social.

Variety also results from many compositional techniques, some of which have been mentioned above. We may further add the interpolated songs, quotations from named and unnamed sources in both prose and verse, and the Latin phrases which usually summarize (often ironically) the sense of a particular scene or description.

Mesonero's style is also tightly organized around a second central principle: clarity. Because the author wrote for publications needing a mass readership and also because of his usual moral purpose—even if diluted at times—it was imperative that the basic objective of each article be clear. Numerous aspects of point of view, style, and structure which promote clarity have been suggested in previous paragraphs. These will not be further elaborated here. It is, however, significant that the vast majority of stylistic traits developed by Mesonero tend toward the promotion of clarity even when their principal expressive justification may be along other lines. A prime example is the frequent exaggeration, the caricature (especially with minor characters), and the trend toward ludicrous or slapstick humor in such articles as *La comedia casera* (*A Stage Play at Home*) and *Madrid a la luna* (*Madrid in the Moonlight*). By over-emphasizing the main lines of the sketch, Mesonero prevents misinterpretation of human or situational meaning while he coincidentally obtains the facile laughter inherent in this type of writing. This simplified concentration also explains Mesonero's preference for typed rather than individualized characterizations.

Throughout the *Scenes of Madrid* the reader notes the recurring employment of contrasts. Distinct epochs, locations, generations, social classes, and value systems are constantly paired one against another for purposes of promoting clear vision of the central issues. It is not infrequent for these expressive juxtapositions to form part of the title: *The Little Hat and the Shawl*, *The Stranger in His Own Country*, and *1802 and 1832*.

A final significant factor in promoting a clear image for the reader is the numerous aspects of what may be termed the techniques of repetitiveness. I do not maintain that all these techniques fit into a stylistic strategy of the author. In some cases, I feel sure that these traits correspond to a natural verboseness and basic lack of inventiveness. The fundamental aspect is, however, the end result. By insisting in diverse articles upon the same character types, the same flaws or virtues in the Spanish character, and by employing a verbose, repetitive, and highly explanatory style, the author assures himself of an informed if not convinced audience. Mesonero's sentences are usually lengthy, but they are broken into relatively short clauses in which explanation, modification, and development of the sentence topic is carried forward. When suggesting examples for particular assertions, it is not infrequent for Don Ramón to present a list. Montesinos has referred to Mesonero as an "inventory-taker or cataloguer of things,"[8] a phrase meant to refer to his descriptive technique but which also illuminates the present subject. Accumulation, enumeration, parallelism (with or without anaphora), parenthetical interpolations, adjectival abundance, circumlocution (often humorous) are all descriptive of Mesonero's style. One can find single sentences which run for an entire paragraph. At times the writer abuses anaphora or a series of rhetorical questions or exclamations beyond the reader's endurance. Repetition and wordiness may aid explanation, but they also dilute stylistic intensity; little direct, dramatic presentation is possible.

The above comments are not to suggest that Don Ramón could not be concise or write with impact. He is most likely to attain strength of expression when describing crowd scenes; in a few words he is often able to suggest the presence of bustling, jostling multitudes; one of his major successes occurs in *La procesión del Corpus* (*The Corpus Christi Procession*).

The prose of Mesonero Romanos is not filled with imagery or frequent appeals to the various human senses. There are several articles which seem exceptional, but the majority are written in a chatty, conversational style with concrete, quotidian terms; the emphasis is on appeals to the intellect and to sight. Some articles, especially those with crowd scenes, also include frequent appeals to hearing. The limited number of similes and metaphors in Mesonero's writings usually has a literary basis; the most common term of comparison is the theater or the work of an actor.

The comments made above relative to the stylistic prolixity of Mesonero may be considered as even more pertinent as one proceeds forward into the second series of the *Scenes of Madrid*. Little by little the reader notes a less dramatic framework and a more prosaic expression. Paralleling this movement is the ever-increasing length of the articles which at times are divided into two, three, or four parts, each portion published on succeeding days. Mesonero conceived of these articles as superior due to their increased philosophic intention, but one might also view them as inferior due to the diminished spontaneity of the prose, and the increased length without an increase in dramatic or creative intensity. There are exceptions of course; the above comments refer only to tendencies. In all fairness, some of Mesonero's most renowned sketches appear at the conclusion of his work: *From the Roof Up, The Newcomer, Requiebros de Lavapiés* (*Love Tales from the Lavapiés District*), and *El Martes de Carnaval y el Miércoles de Ceniza* (*Carnival Tuesday and Ash Wednesday*).

In retrospect, the contribution of Don Ramón to the development of a more direct, conversational, and objective prose was considerable. His object-laden realistic descriptions, his frequent dialogues full of colloquial expressions or language pertinent to the background of the speaker, and the flavor of documentation or direct observation which is present is a direct antecedent of the less rhetorical and oratorical prose of the Realistic novel. It is not without justification that Pérez Galdós, in Chapter Four of *El amigo Manso* (*The Meek Friend*), proposes Jovellanos, Moratín, Mesonero, and Larra as models of modern Spanish prose.

VI *Aspects of Theme and Vision*

The *Scenes of Madrid* is essentially unclassifiable in terms of subject 'matter. Within a governing point of view such as the influence of foreign customs or the transformation of traditional Spanish celebrations, Mesonero quickly illuminates many circumstances and human types. Often, also, he contrasts two epochs such as in *1802 and 1832*. The great number of articles, seventy-one in the edition of 1881, prohibits a detailed account of all the subjects. In any case, many of these are suggested in previous paragraphs; the same topic is also extended in Chapter Six. In a few lines here, I will limit myself to a summary of some underlying constants not treated elsewhere in this study.

The works of "The Curious Chatterbox" principally develop a social and ethical dimension of reality. This writer avoids serious study of religion, politics, economics, or other diverse ideologies. Even within the areas he examines, Mesonero may be described as a superficial thinker with limited interests, at least as he manifests them in his literature. His strength is not profound treatment but vivid portrayal; his mind functions best when focused upon such areas as concrete day-to-day municipal activities, the recollection of past years, or the more routine aspects of literary scholarship. Furthermore, his literary method, which features comic exaggeration and caricature, also effectively prevents him from objective or profound approximations to his themes. His most vivid accounts humorously reveal human flaws, mainly those related to hypocritical behavior, ingenuousness, or colorful fanaticism. It must be observed, however, that Don Ramón's writings, while differing notoriously from those of his beloved Miguel de Cervantes, do resemble those of the latter in that the surface humor only partially masks an aftertaste of quiet sadness. This sadness exists because of the implied moral bankruptcy. A final melancholy pervades even such boisterous articles as *From the Roof Up*. Only in isolated cases such as *La calle de Toledo* (*Toledo Street*) does the author content himself with colorful, animated word pictures with little underlying moral preoccupation. One departs the *Scenes of Madrid* with a vision of a society greatly out of focus. The ostentation, the hypocrisy, the growing materialism are all mirrored against a background of stagnancy and mediocrity. Change is rapid, even dizzying, but it is superficial, skin deep. Foreign models are imitated but not comprehended.

One aspect of the *Scenes of Madrid* has not received proper attention. Don Ramón can be devastatingly critical, foreshadowing in tone and treatment the writings of the Naturalists of the 1880s in Spain. In *Grandeur and Misery* the reader discovers a morally empty marquis who falls prey to his thieving servants (stereotyped Naturalistic exploitation in reverse), finally becoming almost a prisoner of their stratagems. This tendency climaxes in *A Night at Vigil*, an article which reveals insensitivity, stupidity, and corruption on the part of the attending doctors and disloyalty, insincerity, and selfishness on the part of the family and friends of a dying count. The tone is not lightened at the conclusion, a somewhat rare occurrence. Although such harsh treatment is infrequent, the same melancholy related to the ex-

posure of human flaws and evil is present in *The Picture* and
El duelo se despide en la iglesia (*Grief Ends at the Church*),
among many others.

In terms of the social dimension of reality, Mesonero devotes
the greater part of his energies to the blossoming middle class,
especially those trapped in the confusion of the changing social
and economic arrangements. The highly ambitious, superficially
prepared youth and the bewildered, embittered, or entrenched
older generation are all present. Frequently Don Ramón, with or
without another representative of his same age group, critically
observes the affairs of the youth.

In the *Panorama of Madrid* there are numerous lively, inventive
accounts which feature the lower classes of society. Examples
are found in *Jane's Stroll, El barbero de Madrid* (*The Barber
from Madrid*), and *The Old Cape and the Spirited Dance Party*.
The lower class also appears in the second series of sketches, but
generally the treatment is more panoramic than scenic. While
the articles on the middle class predominate numerically, those
that deal with the lower strata are usually more colorful, more
humorous, more vivid. *Toledo Street; Madrid in the Moonlight;*
and *The Boardinghouse, or Spain in Madrid* are all anthology
pieces. Mesonero appears to take advantage of the less fortunate
in that he exploits their speech, customs, and weaknesses for
their entertainment value. It is in these sketches that he most
decisively employs caricature and a sense of the grotesque; this
tendency culminates in *The Newcomer*, an article in which Juan
Algarrobo is described in zoological terms and is alluded to as
"semihuman" and "almost rational."

Don Ramón's reticence with regard to the aristocracy has been
noted in preceding pages. However, his negative attitude is at
times strongly implied, even openly stated in *Las niñas del día*
(*Today's Girls*). The author rarely develops this theme, except
in passing, and when he does he aims at relatively low levels of
nobility. Mesonero's basic values strongly resemble those of the
progressive aristocracy of the eighteenth century. He urges the
marquis of *Grandeur and Misery* to reflect upon the virtues of
direct contact with nature, self-discipline, hard labor, and social
commitment. With all this, Don Ramón views many of the
wealthy and privileged as in a period of decline, of lack of will,

of immorality. Their function is to lead, but their decline has permitted less-prepared elements to fill in the void.

Mesonero's overall vision of early nineteenth-century Spain, then, is surely not optimistic. His natural good humor and knowledge of communicative strategy allowed him to present a festive posture, but rarely does he display human or institutional characteristics worthy of emulation. As his contemporary, Juan E. Hartzenbusch, wrote as early as 1851: "Mesonero desires to improve our customs; therefore he only displays those types whose behavior needs reform; . . . these are the defects from which Spanish society is suffering: what is not in his books is what is already respectable and good."[9]

CHAPTER 6

The Final Sketches

IN 1862 Mesonero Romanos decided to reissue several representative *costumbrista* sketches from the material he had composed since approximately 1840. This final collection is generally known as *Tipos, grupos y bocetos de cuadros de costumbres (Types, Groups and Outlines of Costumbrista Sketches)*; it appeared as a portion of a larger whole which included both series of the *Scenes of Madrid*.[1] Most of these writings had been published previously in journals or books. For example, *La patrona de huéspedes (The Boardinghouse Patroness)*, *El pretendiente (The Government Job Seeker)*, and *Tipos perdidos, tipos hallados (Types Lost, Types Found)* had initially appeared in the important *The Spaniards in a Self-Portrait*.

Critics, as usual, have received this final group of sketches with widely diverse judgments. Sainz de Robles views *Types, Groups and Outlines* as the supreme artistic triumph of its author: "Soft irony, subtle truth, a tendency toward caricature without any lessening of the characters' humanity, precision with respect to the essential traits...."[2] Montesinos continues to observe an increase in discursiveness and moralization and a decrease in creative intensity as "The Curious Chatterbox" ages.[3] Most seem to agree with González López: "...this collection is a consequence of the previous ones, so that, when he [Mesonero] succeeds, he repeats himself, and when he repeats himself, he falls into a certain puerility."[4]

One of the most insightful, informative statements made by Mesonero on his own art serves as a prologue to this work. Called *Adiós al lector (A Farewell to the Reader)*, the title betrays the melancholy, somewhat frustrated dejection of the formerly festive creator of animated prose snapshots. *A Farewell to the Reader* develops several main themes, one of which is

126

the author's failure to follow up his *Scenes of Madrid* with a third, more broadly focused work: "... the satiric and moral painting of contemporary customs and characters, not precisely fixed to the capital city, but stretching across modern Spanish society in general" (II, p. 202). Mesonero sadly excuses himself, pleading increasing age, the inability to create in a calculated manner, and, most significantly, the rapidity with which modern society was becoming transformed: "The road-worn painter confesses himself conquered; the faint-hearted observer feels his vigor and imagination darkened, confused; and in this situation it is incumbent upon the artist to lay down his musty, classical pen" (II, p. 202). In an honest survey of his declining powers, he admits that *Types, Groups and Outlines* is only an appendix or continuation of the *Scenes of Madrid,* even though he once had envisioned for it an independent status.

In spite of the disappointment inherent in these observations, Don Ramón does claim certain values for his third collection: "Possibly by comparing its content with that of previous works the contrast that the author desired to present between these epochs will become more clear; also, possibly the reader may note more philosophical intention in the literary execution even if less spontaneity and dramatic interest" (II, p. 203).

The edition of 1881 which I use for purposes of dividing Mesonero's works separates *Types, Groups and Outlines* into three parts: (1) *Tipos y caracteres* (*Types and Characters*); (2) *Bocetos de cuadros de costumbres* (*Outlines of Costumbrista Sketches*); and (3) *Poesías Típico-Características* (*Some Typical Poems*). Only the first two divisions will be included in this chapter since Mesonero's poetry, including the eleven poems of this work, is discussed in Chapter Three.

There is little doubt that Mesonero's art suffers a notable decline after the *Scenes of Madrid.* However, it must be remembered that the bulk of his energy after 1842 was given to public acts and writings. Historical, civic, biographical, and critical articles will flow from his pen with regularity, but the imaginative dimension diminishes in quantity and quality. One may even perceive the superiority of the sketches written in the 1840s (*The Boardinghouse Patroness*) as opposed to those composed later such as *Un año en Madrid* (*A Year in Madrid*).

The longwinded erudite or simply empty introductions, the numerous undeveloped and unnamed human examples for his theses, the variety of subject matter within a single article, and the lengthy and very obvious summary moralizations all contrast in their lack of intensity with Don Ramón's previous art. A further weakness is an increased repetitiveness; Mesonero leans more and more on subjects and structures he had developed previously, especially in the *Manual of Madrid*. The structure of the month-by-month review of typical activities in Madrid had been employed previously on two occasions before utilized again in *A Year in Madrid*.

The first sketch is entitled *Pobres vergonzantes* (*The Discreet Poor*); many of its characteristics are prototypic of other articles found in this work. The subject is the many people of Madrid who are able to live by their wits, at the expense of others, instead of working. The author does not describe the truly indigent; his interest lies in those who, for one reason or another, follow this path. As he states, "Indigence is for them a way of life" (II, p. 205). The dart of irony pricks many, and the same rapid, superficial narrative glance is characteristic of this third collection. Mesonero finds common to all such folk a lack of shame and a cunning ability to work on others' weaknesses or pride. He depicts the retired military man who, wearing his battle ribbons, calls on his acquaintances at mealtime while making it clear he has not yet dined or enjoyed a cigar. Other "victims of society," including elderly widows (or their daughters) and unemployed politicians or government officials, also cultivate this art. Not all is seen in a light tone. Don Ramón also includes certain young, well-endowed but vicious males who traffic the favors of unfortunate women. After passing review over numerous nameless and undeveloped examples, Don Ramón closes with a moral discourse which includes several quotations from authorities. The intent of *The Discreet Poor* is to cast aspersions upon those who live off the toil and sympathies of others. The author terms these people parasites and disguised beggers. The sketch suffers from an instability of tone and narrative focus. At times, Don Ramón approaches a serious social study; at other moments he indulges in wordy, festive banter or discursive moralization. His numerous examples receive meager development, and the author can be faulted for several poorly selected ones. For instance, who can blame a widow in nineteenth-century Spain for seeking support in any legitimate way? As an example of the interruption of the serious treatment by listlike accumulations of humorous references, we may cite: "These tireless parasites, folk of interminable lives, invited stone statues present at every social gathering, nonpaying spectators at every show, tablemates with all of society, witnesses of every marriage, seconds at every duel-lunch, a piece of furniture in every theater box, necessary operators in every lady's dressing room ..." (II, p. 207). This sentence continues in a similar manner, a syntactic structure found frequently in these articles.

In *Gustos que merecen palos* (*Tastes that Deserve Punishment*), the author ironically surveys various fanatics in miniature, persons who seem eccentric but whose habits concern only those in their immediate social circle. (Mesonero Romanos rarely attacks persons that represent influential forces of social power.) After five paragraphs of introduction in which he describes the topics he will not treat in his article, and in which even he notices his departure from the title subject, Don Ramón views a series of mostly unnamed persons who, depending on one's point of view, can be condemned or praised for their tastes: a widow who lavishes money on dogs and cats; a father and husband who spends most of his time in public or religious affairs; and a scholar totally committed to useless antiquities. Receiving more development is Dorotea Ventosa y Panza-altrote, who, appearing to be charitable because of her fundraising activities, has herself never given money, food, or shelter to the poor. She is more attached to the social prominence gained by contributing time rather than money.

Don Ramón lashes out in this and in other articles at the uneducated but intrepid youths who seek personal gain by joining the forces of government opposition in the newspapers until they are able by threat or intimidation to obtain a position in the establishment themselves. *Tastes that Deserve Punishment* is, in short, rambling, out-of-focus, moralizing, and caught in the confusion between a light, personal tone and a serious, ironic treatment.

The following article, *Industria de la capital* (*Industry of the*

Capital), humorously points to Madrid as a factory of false, unearned reputations. Those who suggest that Spain's capital may be industrially inferior to Barcelona are wrong, as Mesonero ironically demonstrates. Again the theme of sudden success for undeserving youth is developed. A significant feature of *Types, Groups and Outlines* begins to emerge with this article. Mesonero, even though he persists in employing humor, is becoming increasingly bitter in his attacks; his irony approaches sarcasm as he observes: "What are, for example, a machine or a delicately woven cloth produced by the inventiveness and toil of the sons of Barcelona, when seen beside one of our wise court officials, politicians, or writers—all of them improvised with the slightest turn of the great reputation factory of the Puerta del Sol?" (II, p. 220). Besides further brief references to this theme in various sketches, the same idea is elaborated again at length in *El incensario* (*The Incensory*).

An increased bitterness which is best defined as pessimism in several of these articles becomes, then, a new part of Don Ramón's literary personality. He identifies less and less with Madrid after the mid-point of the century. A climactic sketch with regard to Mesonero's bitter criticism of his native land is *Cuatro para un hueso* (*Four for One Bone*). Here the author unfavorably compares the unemployment situation in Spain with that of other Western countries; he even refers to "... this Spain that is coming apart at the seams" (II, p. 276). Parallel with the pessimism is a tone of nostalgia when "The Curious Chatterbox" recalls the days of his youth. This criticism of contemporary life as opposed to a softer treatment of earlier days is easily perceived in those articles in which one time frame is juxtaposed with the other; this occurs, for example, in *The Government Job Seeker* and *Types Lost, Types Found*. In the latter work Don Ramón selects six societal functions which have been transformed during his life span. The underlying unity of each change is a movement towards the social, the political, the worldly, or the material. Mesonero does not hide his negative feelings toward some of these happenings, although the older generation does not escape his irony. Society is now influenced by the political journalist rather than the religious worker; financial wizards now outshine nobles and aristocrats; and youth now concerns itself with future political combinations rather than strutting before the females of Madrid. In a culminating moment of nostalgia, Mesonero, probably recalling his own youth, exclaims: "Oh, young dandy of Madrid! Oh fresh and spicy human type! Where do you hide? Oh available girls! Pray to God that he may return, with his bell-shaped boots and his enormous ties, his ruffled stomacher and his cotton gloves. Pray that he may return, with his flowery illusions and his scanty learning, with his idyls and *ovillejos,* and without beards, newspapers, scepticism, and a governmental instinct" (II, p. 242).

In this work's second division, *Outlines of Costumbrista Sketches,* Mesonero includes seven articles composed between 1840 and 1860. In general these brief sketches, most of them composed close to 1840, are superior to those written later. The writings of *Types, Groups and Outlines* are not arranged in a chronological order. In *El gabán (The Overcoat),* the author cursorily reviews male fashions in Spain, concentrating upon the nineteenth century. Mesonero, throughout his life, had a descriptive predilection for clothing, architecture, and room interiors; he rarely describes a human being in terms of facial or corporal features. In this sketch, he concludes that the history of apparel reveals much of a people's soul:

...now we are living in a period in which no one believes in fashion, just as no one believes in politics, literature, or anything else. An anarchy reigns in sartorial matters, just as it does in our society; poor taste and an unattractive ideal is displayed in clothing, just as in our actions; variety is covered up with cloth, just as empty reasoning with a barrage of rhetoric; finally, all sense of hierarchy has been destroyed, all the classes have been levelled off and mixed together, just as in the social mechanism. Today's society is, therefore, symbolized in the *overcoat.* (II, p. 274)

Mesonero offers another broad social statement in *Las traducciones (The Translations).* The tone is festive in a manner reminiscent of some articles in *Scenes of Madrid.* Finding a widespread, thoughtless imitation of foreign models (especially French) in a host of activities, Mesonero concludes that Spain is "a translated nation" (II, p. 277). After the typical wide-angle introduction, the author becomes more concrete by pondering his future course in this fashionable activity. For various reasons he dismisses the majority of languages: "Italian apparently is only good for music, and even then the charm resides in a poor understanding and a worse pronunciation. English? Oh, English is so thorny; besides, the English people scarcely write any plays, obviously the only worthy literary activity. German, Russian, you try and understand that babble. Portuguese? But what can one translate from Portuguese?" (II, p. 277). Rejecting also the idea of translating bad Spanish translations into better ones ("because first one must be able to comprehend that foolishness" [II, p. 277]), Don Ramón decides to attempt social translations instead. His irony penetrates hypocritical behavior; he translates it into a more truthful rendition. For example, he affirms that when one hears a man speak against the government, one should translate that the gentleman is undoubtedly an unemployed former government employee.

Little new in terms of technique, theme, or style appears in the remaining sketches. In general, Don Ramón's style becomes even more oratorical, his structures more diffuse (in spite of the brevity of these sketches compared to the second series of the *Scenes of Madrid*), and the thematic repetition more obvious. These negative tendencies culminate in *A Year in Madrid,* a pedestrian attempt at characterizing life in the capital according to the month. Repeatedly in *Types, Groups and Outlines* he alludes to the increased politicization of Madrid, the superficiality of learning in the new generation, the lack of objective criticism or commentary in politics or literature, the rapidity with which time passes and society changes, and the degree to which Spain is losing its identity because of servile foreign imitations. Some of these themes become basic in the literature of the succeeding generations, but they are left at the level of simple observations in this work of Don Ramón. Pérez Galdós will profoundly examine people who appear to be something that they are not, and the Generation of 1898, Miguel de Unamuno and Angel Ganivet in particular, will agonize over the problem of Spain's true identity: a sort of culmination of the incipient loss of identity that "The Curious Chatterbox" noted with regard to foreign imitations.

In spite of his growing sternness, Mesonero Romanos continues to present a more serene posture than most of the polemical writers of his day. He does not entirely lose his sense of humor, and he demonstrates himself capable of viewing both sides of many matters. His comments about the women of Madrid, bullfighting, religious friars, and his city's boardinghouses may be chosen as examples. Outspoken and increasingly bitter with respect to political developments, Don Ramón is still, in overall terms, even-tempered.

Types, Groups and Outlines is not a major work. Except for the increased attention to the human type as opposed to the *costumbrista* scene, it does not reveal important new aspects of any dimension of Mesonero's art. The work serves today principally as a historical record; it reveals the complex social and economic transition circa 1850. Those accustomed to the way of a previous generation or to slower development were confused and embittered.

CHAPTER 7

The Memoirs of Don Ramón

AFTER 1850 it is not infrequent to find references in Mesonero's writings to his increasing age, his disappearing creative imagination, and his failing powers of expression. While part of this parallels the same pose of humility that he always assumed, a good share of it is borne out by the increasingly repetitive, verbose, and prosaic quality of his writings. Part of his motivation to undertake another book—published in his seventy-seventh year—must have been a strong desire to relive and, in some sense, preserve *his* world, only remnants of which still existed. There is evidence that he did not identify too closely with postrevolution (1868) Spain, although he had worked diligently in preceding years for progress and change. A large portion of his last years was dedicated to his historical and biographical writings—he was the official chronicler of Madrid—and to orally reliving the past with such young writers as Benito Pérez Galdós. He was proud of his country's advances, but had closer spiritual ties with Isabeline Spain.

A second, related motive for the *Memoirs* was the encouragement by his friends with whom he shared his tales of former times. Don Ramón refers to "... the seductive insistence of his friends and colleagues in literary circles" (V, p. 1). Apparently the strongest force of all was the example and personal intervention of Pérez Galdós. Mesonero admits that all his life he desired to write a satirical novel about early nineteenth-century public life in Spain. He proposed the example of *Gil Blas de Santillana* for his work. Fear of political reprisal as a youth and knowledge of his creative limitations as an adult prevented the fulfillment of his dream. However, when Galdós began to recapture the intimate tone of life of that period in the *Episodios nacionales* (*National Episodes*), Mesonero was stirred to activity. Both the *Memoirs* and the published correspondence between Galdós and Mesonero carry many expressions of admiration and of encouragement in this regard, demonstrating that their influence upon one another was reciprocal. An example is provided by the words of Galdós: "It is important that you persevere in your efforts on the *Memoirs of a Septuagenarian* according to the plan that you were kind enough to show me, so that we all may admire in all its vastness this bold effort of ingenuity, of style, and of memory which will live as long as its sisters, the *Scenes of Madrid.*"[1]

A second concrete stimulus for the *Memoirs* has been revealed by a letter from Don Ramón to Patricio de la Escosura.[2] In early 1876 Escosura published a series of biographical articles on certain nineteenth-century figures such as Espronceda, Ventura de la Vega, and Olózaga. The articles were entitled *Recuerdos literarios* (*Literary Remembrances*), and published in *La Ilustración Española y Americana*. In his letter Mesonero congratulated Escosura, also informing him of a similar work that the former had long planned to write. Instead of concentrating upon famous figures, Mesonero desired to re-create the contours of an entire period, using his "superior memory" as the fundamental source. At the conclusion, however, Don Ramón directly stated that he must renounce his plan as too ambitious for his advanced age and failing talents. Nevertheless, in the same year and in the same journal Mesonero published one article, and in 1877 another, both of which would later form chapters of his *Memoirs.* By 1880 he had taken even stronger resolve, publishing one by one in *La Ilustración* the articles which would later that year form chapters of his *Memoirs.*

Mesonero's *Memoirs* covers the years between 1808 and 1850. In the prologue the author clearly states his purpose:

. . . he [Mesonero] only intends to occupy himself with those details that, because of their insignificance or their connection with intimate, private life, do not fit into the normal historical framework, but that usually are, nevertheless, quite pertinent for giving it [history] character and color.

These purely anecdotal details can only be elucidated by an actual witness of the events, one who is born with them, grows and develops alongside them, and who aspires to truthfully and directly sketch the men and objects that existed, as well as the contemporary opinions that he managed to overhear. (V, p. 1)

In keeping with his well-known desire for privacy, Mesonero treats his material from the point of view of a second row observer. Even when describing events in which he directly intervened, he seldom places himself in the center of the narration. The work is divided into two main parts, the first covering the years between 1808 and 1823, the second from 1824 to 1850. This division is quite arbitrary. A better division, corresponding with the material itself, would place the concluding date for the first part at 1833. For the years between 1808 and 1833 (basically the period of the War of Independence and the reign of Ferdinand VII) Mesonero emphasizes politics, using references to himself only to elucidate public realities. Frequently he allows his political and historical judgments (tinged with moralism) to be felt. This part of the work is proportionately longer than the other, and is written in a more lively, creative style than the second portion. The second division of the work can itself be subdivided: the first half centers mostly upon literary and other cultural material, the second half upon Mesonero's intervention in municipal reform. The author depicts his own achievements and experiences more directly than in the previous section.

Mesonero begins his *Memoirs* with the transcendent events of March 19, 1808. On that date public riots forced the flight of Godoy, the queen's favorite and, in effect, the head of state. Soon thereafter the French invaded, and several years of war commenced. Mesonero intentionally filters these experiences through the consciousness of a five year old in order to better dramatize them, and give them an original hue.

The book begins *in medias res*: the regular family prayers are violently interrupted by sudden flashes, loud noises, and enthusiastic political chants. Don Ramón quickly establishes a groundwork of self-deprecating humor in order to charm the reader and distance himself from the immediacy of a serious moment in Spanish history. He recalls that one of the chants was "¡Muera el Choricero!" ("Death to the sausage maker!"). Thinking that this ominous expression referred to Mr. Peña, the family's sausage merchant, little Ramón asked his parents what harm Peña had done. His father quickly informed him that the sausage maker was Godoy, not Peña. Mesonero again blundered by calling Godoy the "Prince of Peace" instead of the "Prince of Darkness" which his father preferred. To compound his error and the humor of the scene, the boy innocently sang a schoolboy jingle in praise of Godoy. The incident concluded with a reproval from the senior Mesonero.

The evocation of this past world continues in a similar vein. Mesonero links significant events with minor, intimate details. We live a large portion of the revolution from inside the family's house, hearing shots and other threatening noises, and listening to the family's private and social conversation. The author recalls that he fell, seriously cutting his head, the moment the initial shots rang out; the family's sense of emergency is thus doubled, and is well captured by the author. Confusing rumors are rampant, and the reader is allowed to hear them, thus further dramatizing the narrative perspective. By this means Mesonero re-creates the vital experience of such important days in Spanish history. This is his announced intention, and one that he successfully fulfills in the first half of the *Memoirs*.

Apart from personal and public anecdotes, the author incorporates many poems, songs, and other refrains then popular, directly related to the ebb and flow of Spanish-French relations. Some of them are patriotic, others are humorous—even salacious at times. Together they successfully suggest the public mentality, especially with regard to Joseph Bonaparte, the imposed chief of state. For the period following the War of Independence, Mesonero includes popular verse forms to suggest the growing chasm between liberals and traditionalists. A sense of being on the inside of events is increased by this technique.

Space limitations prohibit a detailed summary of the content of the *Memoirs*. In his work the author views public and private events as they occur. A chronological structure underpins most of the narrative, except in certain situations where expository logic requires otherwise. For example, Mesonero's private travels to Salamanca in 1818 are combined with a previous family trip there in 1813; this preserves the unity of the experience, and allows for a contrastive description of a place ravaged by war in 1813 and quite recovered in 1818.

Particular emphasis is given to the epoch of the War of Independence and the restoration of Ferdinand VII (1808–1814), the triennium of constitutional government and free thinking (1820–1823), and the interesting years between 1827 and 1836 when Mesonero commenced his literary activities, foreign travels, journalistic enterprises, and public service intervention. For this latter period, he colorfully describes the coming of Romanticism—especially as related to the theater—highlighting the numerous literary and cultural societies of the period.

The book is many things, and this diversity lies at the heart of the genre. It would be difficult if not impossible to formulate a precise definition of the "memoir" form. At its basis is a narration of past events directly experienced or witnessed by the writer. Mesonero takes full advantage of the openness of his form. The multiformity of his work is evident as the reader moves from section to section, contrasting both content and narrative technique. In terms of content, at times the *Memoirs* approximates a standard recitation of public history, such as when relating the events of 1820 preparatory to constitutional government. Frequently, however, Mesonero's particular perspective, with his employment of previously unnoticed details and anecdotes, serves to vitalize this type of reminiscence.

At other moments, with the emphasis still on politics, the work takes on a more intimate, almost novelistic quality. Don Ramón ushers the reader into the chambers of the King and his ministers, allowing a direct view of the plotting of these power-hungry men. Ferdinand's regular purges of his consorts due to his distrust of everyone are witnessed firsthand. The long narrative of the author's months in the National Militia in 1823 is not unlike a picaresque novel in places. One critic has even suggested that a certain amount of fictive embellishment may indeed be present, without, of course, sacrificing the basic truth of the account.[3]

Another segment of the work's content is given over to the author's own experiences. As mentioned, up to his period of literary beginnings, Mesonero normally draws on his own life solely to elucidate public realities. The trip to Salamanca does not feature the author alone; emphasized instead are the emotional anguish of his father at seeing such widespread destruction and some brief descriptions of fallen buildings and human suffering. One of the subtle expressive achievements of the work comes forth in these few pages. Many Spaniards, having faced in previous years so many scenes of suffering and death, had apparently become hardened, even insensitive, to many aspects of war. Mesonero recounts how he and many children played several days with the bones and skeletons of the dead soldiers, at times piling and burning them for fertilizer at the insistence of the local peasants. The effect of this and other similar experiences communicates a vision of an unconsciously brutalized society. The torture of political enemies, the mass murders of clergymen, these and other tales are sometimes recounted in a relatively colorless manner which serves implicitly to suggest this insensitivity. Mesonero does not condone crime or violence as an adult—quite the opposite. But his reactions are somewhat cooly moralistic; missing is a degree of emotional outrage. A notable exception occurs in his treatment of the drunken, bribed masses which violently intimidated the liberals several times in Ferdinand's behalf. For these unconscious zealots Mesonero holds nothing but contempt.

The author's esthetic creed also cools these pages. In his all-inclusive search for fairness and objectivity, Mesonero often represses his own personality. He is able (commendably) to point to several positive achievements of men who have just undergone the rigors of his criticism. The author's treatment of King Ferdinand and his minister Calomarde are prime examples.

In the second half of the *Memoirs*, Mesonero's autobiography more directly fills the pages rather than serving larger purposes as before. Justifiably proud of his writings, his civic and cultural accomplishments, and his founding of *El Semanario Pintoresco Español*, the author comes more to center stage in the final third of the book. He presents himself almost as a social prophet at the conclusion, reproducing contemporary testimony to his own achievements.

However, even in this portion Mesonero often slips into the background; it is here that a fourth division of the work's content —literary history and criticism—may be established, although this material was present to a lesser degree earlier. The paucity and inferiority of writers previous to 1833 is repeatedly treated, as is the cause: political repression and ignorant censorship. The beginnings of Romanticism and *costumbrismo,* the creation of many literary coteries, the influences of one writer upon another, and the development of drama after King Ferdinand all figure importantly in the work's final pages.

We have seen, then, that politics, military affairs, the economy, social progress, literary and other cultural matters, and certain portions of the author's autobiography are neatly intertwined to form a coherent whole. Mesonero has taken full advantage of the flexibility of his literary form to produce a work which by its own inner diversity tends to maintain reader interest. Its appeal to the historian relates to the material itself; its appeal to the general reader is partly an outgrowth of its careful, varied construction.

Diversity is not a function of content alone. Certain allusions to literary techniques have already been made earlier in this chapter. Apart from those mentioned, we may point to Mesonero's control over tone. So as to coincide with the shifting events of history, the author can be festive, ironic, sarcastic, objective, or pathetically tragic. Playful tunes and refrains are juxtaposed with the human tragedy of the 1811–1812 famine. The author's intellectually expansive foreign travels and early literary successes are counterposed with the quietly sad presentation of the cholera epidemic of 1834, the death of his mother (who attended Don Ramón herself), and the violence of the hate-filled masses against the clergy. Effectively captured is the rhythm of life itself—the ebb and flow of joy and sorrow. The already mentioned accounts of the childhood games with the bones of the war dead is a stark example of how the author could combine such disparate notions as the innocence of childhood and the brutal realities of war. A widely appealing gamut of emotions is present in the *Memoirs,* although understatement is the most employed narrative voice.

Mesonero repeatedly insists, both in text and footnotes, on the veracity of his presentation. He asserts that his role is that of a humble photographer who captures the truth about facts and men (V, p. 1). Even though this insistence carries the danger of arousing the reader's suspicions, normally the presentation serves to support these claims. The author reproduces from memory or documents the details of particular scenes and conversations,[4] and also includes inventorylike lists of dates, theatrical plays presented in certain years, and the participants in diverse activities. The copious footnotes—carrying statistics, explanatory material, and further anecdotes—also give the appearance of authority. Also blending into this whole is the partly faceless and usually humble narrator who reduces his presence by concentrating upon exterior realities. In this manner the appearance of subjectivity is lessened. His claims to relative insignificance in the society of his time make him an unpretentious personality with whom the general reader can easily identify. The chatty style, light irony, and frequent humor all work for this same end. The tendency is, then, to accept his word as reliable. The most eloquent testimony as to the actual truthfulness of the *Memoirs* is found in the numerous cases of its use as documentation for historians.[5]

A noteworthy stylistic accomplishment is the skill with which Mesonero captures the animation of crowd scenes. Whether in celebration or in riot, the author fixes upon movement, sights, sounds, smells, and color, making an impressive sensorial display. Successfully communicated by Don Ramón's descriptions are the joy in Madrid during Ferdinand's first entry into the city on March 24, 1808, and after the first forced exit of the French during the War of Independence; the intimidating riots after the return of Ferdinand in 1814 and 1823; and the raging mobs that burned convents and slaughtered religious workers in 1834. Of the legacies the author passed on to the Realistic novel, the crowd scene technique may be one of the most significant.

Mesonero, throughout his literary career, utilized himself as one of his most basic sources. His propensity for restating or enlarging that which he had already written is a stylistic constant. In the *Memoirs* this is one of the most fundamental structural facts, but it seems quite natural, even necessary, given the purpose of the work. Detailed summaries of several of the long reform-oriented writings are presented, and certain chapters given to description, especially Chapter 10 of Part One, are similar to parts of *Ancient Madrid*. Also repeated is a newspaper article dealing with an interesting interview the author enjoyed with Manuel Godoy in Paris some thirty years after the latter's fall from power. The *Memoirs* concludes with the reproduction of a long poem written in 1845 which proclaims every facet of the author's independence—economic, social, intellectual—of which he was so boastfully proud. Previously in the work he had included three other of his poems which related to political circumstance.

Also typical of the author's customary style is the avoidance of prolonged treatment of negative societal aspects. This is not to say that Don Ramón glosses over the truth, or distorts reality. Many examples of brutality, corruption, and ignorance are adduced in his book. In fact, as an elderly man Mesonero seems more candid and bold than ever. His historical judgments, political opinions, and evaluations of public personalities are surprisingly frank. The fact is, however, that the author prefers not to dwell at length on these areas, or treat them profoundly. They are superficially recognized and no more. He saves his detail for descriptions of places, events, customs, and the narration of anecdotes.

In spite of the normally rapid treatment of public issues, there are several notable exceptions in the *Memoirs*. A strong independent judgment is demonstrated by the author's attempt to revise Spanish opinion toward Manuel Godoy and Joseph Bonaparte, both unpopular figures. With respect to the former, Mesonero includes an interview in which the "Prince of Peace" is treated sympathetically; Godoy's attempts to modernize techniques in elementary education are especially appreciated. Joseph Bonaparte is seen as a hard-working, progressive leader who was unfairly slandered during his time in Madrid. In both cases, as with the comments relative to Ferdinand VII, Don Ramon presents a rounded viewpoint, insisting upon the positive aspects when few if any previous commentators had done so.

As suggested, an aura of moralism and didacticism sometimes pervades the strict objectivity which the author had proposed to achieve. This stylistic trait of Don Ramón partly explains his avoidance of detailed probings into criminality or violence. José Perlado has commented upon literary structure, noting that the chapters normally commence with descriptions, scenes, or other events, and gradually move toward concluding reflections which have normally dispassionate ethical overtones.[6] This mixture of social focus, emphasis on objective details and facts, and moralistic judgment by the narrator is another aspect of Mesonero's writings which appears intact in the Spanish novel of Realism.

From his comfortable and independent middle class viewpoint, then, Mesonero Romanos has carefully constructed a hybrid fabric which joins with the memoirs of Alcalá-Galiano to represent the maximum nineteenth-century achievement in the genre. The author's personal prestige, the drama inherent in the material itself, the conscious artistic manipulation of the materials, and the warm, unpretentious style combine to explain the success of the *Memoirs*. When Mesonero criticizes, he normally does not offend; when he praises, he avoids adulation. His works have wide appeal in a country still torn by ideological division, a fact explicable in part by his concentration upon the detail of common daily realities rather than wide social panoramas. His ability to transcend factionalism and briefly unite differing peoples in the enjoyment and instruction of his work is a major portion of the definition of Mesonero's style.

CHAPTER 8

Miscellaneous Works

DON Ramón de Mesonero Romanos' place in the literary
history of Spain deservedly rests upon his *costumbrista*
articles and his *Memoirs of a Septuagenarian*. However, to
complete the picture of this multifaceted literary personality, it
is important to examine, albeit briefly, many lesser writings. Precise classification is not always possible, but for expository purposes these works are divisible into travel memoirs, literary criticism and erudition, and historical-descriptive miscellanea.

I *The Travel Writings*

Although the most significant results of Mesonero's travels
were his writings and personal involvement in municipal
reform, he also published one book and several articles which
together can be called travel memoirs. Only those writings which
dwell on journeys to places some distance from Madrid will be
considered in this category.

In early August, 1833, Mesonero left Madrid on a trip which
did not conclude until May of 1834. His route allowed him to
spend time in such cities as Valencia, Barcelona, Marseilles,
Toulon, Lyon, Paris, London, Manchester, Liverpool, and Birm-
ingham. As a result he published several articles, mainly in his
El Semanario Pintoresco Español, on such subjects as the burial
of a French Romantic playwright named Victor Ducange; the
debut of a play by Victor Hugo; impressions of his first day in
Paris; descriptions of both the cathedral of Notre Dame of Paris
and London's Westminster Abbey; and a narrative of his return
to Madrid from Paris.

Apparently Mesonero originally planned to write a complete
description of his first foreign travels, but only a fragment was
completed. His sons documented this intention when they pub-

144

lished the fragment and a long, carefully plotted outline of this projected work.[1] The only concluded portion describes Valencia and Barcelona. Mesonero was enchanted by Valencia; his impressions are animated, suggestive, and demonstrate his natural affinity for the people and the area. His prolonged stay in Valencia during another trip ten years later indicates similar feelings.

Don Ramón was sincerely impressed by the industriousness of the Catalonian people, but he found several of their attitudes distressing. Instead of the warm, casual life style of Valencia, he perceived an aloofness and a feeling of superiority. Don Ramón was forced inconveniently to visit many offices and officials merely because he had forgotten to sign his passport. He writes of the regionalistic pride which causes a Spaniard from another province to feel as though he were a foreigner. The economic questions of free trade and protectionism are alluded to, and Mesonero finds little justification for most of the ideas defended in Barcelona. The people there demanded that other Spanish cities purchase products fabricated in Barcelona, but Mesonero responded that this was a dead question since products from that city already filled the shelves of shops over most of Spain. At this point the sequential narration ends; only the separately published articles mentioned above give further reference to the first trip.

Mesonero's second foreign journey forms the basis for his book *Recuerdos de viaje por Francia y Bélgica en 1840 y 1841* (*Memoirs of a Journey Through France and Belgium in 1840 and 1841*). This work was originally published in the author's illustrated magazine in 1841, then republished in book form later the same year. Three of its chapters are reprints of previously written articles about the first trip to France. There is no description of England in its pages.

In the second trip Mesonero approached France from a different route. Passing through Burgos, Vitoria, and Irún, he was able to gain firsthand information about these wartorn areas. Don Ramón's sympathetic treatment of these places which had recently been the focus of Carlism is noteworthy; an indirect vision of his equanimity and love for all of Spain is evident: his discussion is founded on human rather than ideological terms.

From Irún, he travelled to France, passing through Bayonne, Bordeaux, Tours, and Paris. After arriving in Belgium, Don Ramón made a point of seeing almost all the major cities, especially Brussels, Antwerp, Ostend Ghent, Liège, and Bruges. He returned to Madrid in the spring of 1841.

Many pages of *Memoirs of a Journey* are given to the actual moments of travel. The difficulties, especially those encountered leaving Spain, are alluded to in an ironically humorous tone. It is clear that the author enjoyed immensely the human associations briefly formed while travelling. In a manner similar to that of the *Scenes of Madrid,* he portrays the pretentious characters, the amorous intrigues, and the various accidents and inconveniences encountered on such trips. While travelling in France, Mesonero finds the service more efficient, the inns and hotels more attractive, but the personal associations more difficult to form. In Belgium, all his efforts go toward description and praise of the impressive railroad network which had recently been installed.

With respect to Paris, Mesonero dwells on his initial impressions, the shops and downtown crowds, the major monuments and public buildings, the scientific and literary establishment, the quaint, almost humorous burial of a flamboyant playwright named Victor Ducange, and the theaters and other forms of recreation available to the populace. The author finds many things to praise: the progressive economic and social organization, the energy and superior intelligence of the people, the modern cemeteries, and the flourishing artistic and literary world. Abundant detail is advanced regarding the same subjects that will interest him during his later years on the City Council. The configuration of the houses, streets, and sidewalks is noted, as are garbage collection, street lighting, philanthropic associations, and much more. In general, Mesonero finds almost every aspect of the social structure praiseworthy.

However, whenever Mesonero treats elements which might be loosely termed "spiritual," he usually finds Spain superior to France. He prefers Spain's churches, art, dances, and also feels more affinity for his country's form of family life. Finding the Frenchman too cold and materialistic, he feels drawn to the spontaneous warmth and generosity of the Spaniard. Neither is the dark, humid climate of Paris as appealing to him as the warm, clear skies of Madrid. Particularly distasteful to Don Ramón is the horde of French writers who rapidly tour Spain and exploit its exoticism by sending back false, insulting impressions for publication; this theme is repeatedly developed.

One of the structural constants of *Memoirs of a Journey* is the frequent comparisons which the author draws between the realities he encounters while travelling and those of his own country. Again his objectivity and equanimity are evident. Never blind to Spain's weaknesses and always ready to praise the advantages of others, Mesonero is seeking for Spain a synthesis of the best of both worlds. With an implicit trust in man's perfectability and in the Spanish character, our author searches for the external improvements which would bring his native city up to the standards of other European capitals. Although the narrative focus generally rests upon the foreign countries he visits, the soul of Mesonero's travel writings is Spain.

The author frequently halts the forward movement of his work to allude to his mother country. He recalls Spain's poor roads and communications, the threat to personal security while travelling, the unacceptable inns and hotels, the need for improved sanitation, and the lack of tolerance and good manners in many rural areas. A most interesting intercalated essay on the oppressive conditions tolerated by the Spanish female is triggered by a brief observation on French women. Mesonero argues for education, job opportunities, and equal treatment for Spain's women. He lists the many disadvantages found in the latter's situation, noting that sexual discrimination is general in Spain and must end. He concludes by encouraging the female to not fear her own liberation, as it is a fact of life in northern Europe.

The pages dedicated to Belgium are less vigorous. Lengthy descriptions of buildings, monuments, and railroads are normally laudatory in tone. The author makes frequent references to sites which figured in Spain's long presence in Flanders during previous centuries. He admires the people's energy, dedication, and good taste, and finds the railroad system and the hotels to be superior to anything in Europe. Mesonero was keenly aware of the potential boredom in so much description, and refers to the problem in the text. He attempts to condense and be selective as much as possible.

As always, Mesonero employs a variety of literary techniques, especially while describing his stay in France. The descriptions are interrupted by dialogue and first person narration. Don Ramón also utilizes much interior movement—a constantly changing narrative and descriptive perspective—in order to provide variety for the reader. The stroll technique is continued to the same degree as in the *Scenes of Madrid*. Mesonero includes a poem he wrote, humorously describes types and scenes, and dramatizes his descriptions frequently. The style is fluid, spontaneous, almost conversational. Also continued is the writer's tendency to discuss his own work while writing it; frequently the problems of structure and style are discussed. His statement of purpose is concise, and provides an excellent view of the limited purposes of his work:

> Given this fact, the reader should not seek in these paragraphs either methodical description, artistic or literary sketches, pure or anecdotal history, heavy doses of bitter satire, or constant pretexts to provoke silly laughter. Well then, what is this book all about? Very little. A few personal observations, several impartial comparisons, a little temperate criticism, some possibly useful information, certain almost unconnected happenings, and, all in all, an attempt (even though a weak one) to pay the obligatory tribute that everyone owes in all his actions to his native country. (V, p. 263)

On the whole, *Memoirs of a Journey* is pleasurable reading. Common sense, an attempt at fairness and objectivity, and careful observation are at the core of the work. The emotional dimension is subdued; not to be found are deeply personal esthetic reactions to the cities, monuments, or the art. Neither does the writer probe the psychological and spiritual complexities of the people and places he visits. In this sense, Mesonero limits himself to rather superficial appraisals. However, a definite social and historical emotion is felt at certain moments, making these travel memoirs somewhat unique. The details of daily life, the advances in urban affairs, and the historical significance of many sites in Belgium fill the writer with an enthusiasm which is conveyed to the reader.

The final piece of travel writing is also a fragment, similar to the piece described above relative to Mesonero's first trip abroad. On April 2, 1843, Don Ramón and his close friend Francisco de Acebal y Arratia departed Madrid for an extensive journey first to the South, then to the eastern part of Spain. After spending Holy Week in Seville, they travelled throughout the major cities of the southern and eastern coast, finally returning from Valencia to Madrid at the end of October. As they journeyed, they witnessed many of the turbulent events of the revolution of 1843 in which Espartero fell from power.

Don Ramón planned to describe this entire trip, but, as previously, only concluded one portion, that relative to the journey between Madrid and Seville and his stay in the latter city. The work is entitled *Viaje de los dos donceles* (*Travels of Two Well-Born Lads*).[2] Written in a flippant style which attempts also to imitate the archaic language of ancient *cronicones* (brief chronicles), this article holds little significance in a definition of Mesonero's prose. The best-sustained theme is the contrast the author finds between the sumptuous interiors of Seville's houses and buildings, and the simple exteriors and dirty, narrow, twisting streets.

II *Literary Criticism and Erudition*

Mesonero's literary scholarship does not correspond to a particular part of his life; he published an article on translations in 1828, and continued in this vein until days before his death. Nor is it possible to precisely identify those works that may be classified in this category. Don Ramón habitually wove his artistic appreciations into the fabric of his *costumbrista* essays, his biographical sketches, and his travel writings. In fact, numerous pages of his *Memoirs of a Septuagenarian* summarize and extend the literary criticism published previously. Mesonero rarely separated textual analysis from his writings in literary biography and history. Normally these three aspects are combined, the latter two far exceeding the former in quantity.

The impressive amount of these writings is partially explained by remembering that Mesonero wrote regularly for the periodical press for thirty years. Faced with deadlines and having a sincere interest (although limited theoretical preparation) in literary scholarship, he often composed short reviews of plays and of other recent publications. Certain works of Hartzenbusch, Bretón de los Herreros, Roca de Togores, and Gil y Zárate receive his attention repeatedly. The sheer bulk and limited significance of these writings preclude their discussion here; of some significance, however, are articles on literary translations, on *La tía fingida* (*The Fake Aunt*) in which Mesonero sustains the theory of Cervantes' authorship, on the "lamentable" situation of the French novel about 1840 (his criticism is on moral grounds), on Alarcón's *De Madrid a Nápoles* (*From Madrid to Naples*), on the wit of Quevedo and his own indebtedness to this source, and on Washington Irving's *Crónica de la conquista de Granada* (*Chronicle of the Conquest of Granada*). These articles and others can be found today in the two volumes of *Uncollected Works*. Many others remain buried in the pages of the *Revista Española* and *El Semanario Pintoresco Español*.

The vast majority of Mesonero's energy was given to the theater, especially to that of the seventeenth century. The four years in which he adapted and staged plays from Spain's Golden Age are discussed in earlier chapters. Mesonero's critical writings on this topic date from 1829 when he published an article—summarized in Chapter Three—on the theoretical aspects of *rifacimenti*. Between 1837 and 1850 he published three articles on Tirso de Molina, always a favorite subject, and during the span 1851–1853 he studied Moreto, Rojas, Alarcón, Calderón, Mira de Amescua, Mendoza, Solís, Vélez de Guevara, Guillén de Castro, and others.

Even previously, in 1842, Mesonero had published a long study entitled *Rápida ojeada sobre la historia del teatro español* (*Brief Review of the History of the Spanish Theater*). Dividing the material into four parts and depending principally upon the work of other critics, especially L. F. de Moratín, Agustín de Rojas, Nicolás Antonio, Cervantes, and Lope de Vega, Mesonero methodically traces the subject from its liturgical beginnings to his own time. Routine biographical material and time-tested critical appreciations abound. However, at times Mesonero is capable of independent judgment—even surprise. These moments normally relate to negative pronouncements based on Mesonero's rigid moralism. He uses strong language to condemn the theater of Cervantes, several aspects of Lope's works, and even the tendency toward salaciousness in Tirso de Molina.

Another surprising aspect for those who would routinely categorize Mesonero as a Neoclassic critic is his blanket condemnation of eighteenth-century drama until the time of Jovellanos and L. F. de Moratín. In several articles, Mesonero shows himself more of an eclectic critic than a strict Neoclassicist. Although never free from rigid moralism, Mesonero was not servilely bound to the doctrine of unities or to that of literal verisimilitude. His eclecticism increases as he ages.

Don Ramón made an important contribution by discovering that Hurtado de Mendoza's *El marido hace mujer y el trato muda costumbre* (*Husbands Fashion Their Wives and Experience Changes Habits*) was the model for Molière's *L'ecole des maris* (*The School for Husbands*) and not *La discreta enamorada* (*The Clever Woman in Love*) by Lope de Vega. Also, after claiming his incapacity to judge critically the theater of his own epoch, Mesonero takes courage and urges modern writers to abandon their flight from reality and their refuge in fantasy, history, and melodrama; instead, Mesonero suggests:

To study dominant passions; to follow men in their public life; to witness the struggle of unchained ambitions, of scattered memories, of disappearing illusions; to note how time-honored customs are changed, and how old vices are given new names; to tear off, in short, man's modern mask, and cast him in the eternal mirror of truth, the mirror of Cervantes and Molière; all this is what we see as being the present-day task of the dramatist. . . .[3]

Coming at the high tide of Romanticism, this statement clearly suggests just how strongly Mesonero's mentality, if not his art, resembled that which the novelists of Spain's moralistic Realism would soon embrace.

All these studies on the Golden Age were enlarged and adapted to serve as the critical-biographical introductions to five volumes of seventeenth- and early eighteenth-century drama which Mesonero edited for the *Biblioteca de Autores Españoles* between 1857 and 1861.[4] Two volumes highlight the works of lesser known playwrights contemporary to Lope de Vega, two are dedicated to writers after Lope, and one is given to the theater of Francisco de Rojas Zorrilla. In all he edited 154 plays. The introductions are routine; little critical or analytical material is presented. Praise or condemnation is normally done in a vague, subjective manner. Characteristic of much of Mesonero's literary research is the extended chronological and alphabetical catalogue of Golden Age authors and their complete works. This useful catalogue makes up part of the introductory material to three volumes of the five done by Mesonero.

In 1848 Mesonero published a curious and little known anthology on Tirso de Molina.[5] A critical discourse precedes these 303 pages of stories, dialogues, maxims, epigrams, and other humorous miscellanea. The introduction offers little new material, reflecting basically the author's previous research on Tirso. The most noteworthy aspect is a visible movement away from the Neoclassic rules as a critical criterion: "But by means of this same freedom and independence, it is possible that he [Tirso] was able to ascend to the prodigious heights that he reached, heights which are very difficult to attain along the narrow path of scholarly rules."[6] With his concentrated efforts on Tirso, Mesonero was joining Don Dionisio Solís in the attempt to revive general interest in this Golden Age writer who, during the eighteenth century, had been virtually forgotten.

Literary biography was another of Mesonero's strong interests. One article on Nicolás Fernández de Moratín and four on his famous son Leandro demonstrate the spiritual kinship which Mesonero always felt for this family. These studies span the years 1841 to 1882. In addition, numerous paragraphs in the text and notes of Mesonero's *Manual of Madrid* and his *Ancient Madrid* are devoted to the Moratín family, especially to Leandro. A laudatory poem on the occasion of the latter's death was penned in 1829. Don Ramón dedicates other major articles to Diego Rabadán, Hartzenbusch, Góngora, Rita Luna, Vicente García de la Huerta, and, in the same vein, traces the founding and purposes of *El Ateneo, El Liceo,* and his journal *El Semanario Pintoresco Español.* Biography, literary history, and textual analysis are combined in these works. In the article on Rita Luna, the author manifests more psychological penetration than usual, and his comments on García de la Huerta demonstrate some originality of thought as well as a large dose of fair-mindedness and equanimity.

On May 17, 1838, Mesonero read his acceptance address before the Royal Spanish Academy, following his election to the post of honorary member, a designation changed to regular status in 1847.[7] This piece of creative literary history is a curious elaboration of the history of the novel as judged by a patriotic moralist. After expounding on the insufficiency of pure genius and creative imagination in literature and the need to temper these qualities with careful, reasoned study, Mesonero sets the foundation of his argument by stating that the goal of any author should be ". . . to educate his fellow man and to improve the condition of his character."[8] He divides the novel into three possible types: (1) the fantastic or marvelous novel, (2) the novel of customs, and (3) the historical or traditional novel. Mesonero affirms that the simple fables of primitive peoples were soon exaggerated, a development which gave rise to bizarre tales in the chivalrous novel. After the redemption of novelistic sanity by Cervantes, the world enjoyed the novel of customs, a novel that paints a true picture of men and society. Soon, however, the picaresque and sentimental novels corrupted the tale of customs. Don Ramón strenuously objects to the picaresque mode on moral grounds, and claims the sentimental tale has too narrow a focus to be considered true.

Our author continues his thesis, arguing that Walter Scott, as Cervantes had done previously, rescued the novel by popularizing historical fiction. Unfortunately, Scott's successors could only pervert the original in a manner similar to the imitative writers of the post-Baroque period. Since the modern novel, especially in France, was morally bankrupt and stylistically insincere, Mesonero encourages Spain's writers to remember *Don Quijote* and *Gil Blas,* and to return to the national tradition. He proposes a hybrid form which would combine categories two and three; the result would be a wide-angle view of contemporary society with an emphasis on verisimilitude. This proposal, the most reasoned portion of the thesis, anticipates the social realism of later decades.

Many obvious objections to Mesonero's presentation are possible. Chronology has been distorted, the moralistic base upon which the argument rests may be challenged, and the lack of examples is distressing. For example, Don Ramón fails to mention which novels compose the supposed golden period of the novel of customs after *Don Quijote*. Would it not be possible to view the picaresque and sentimental novels as new categories rather than illegitimate sons of the novel of customs? Mesonero, in later decades, demonstrates increased eclecticism and historical tolerance. The tendency to label each literary manifestation as "right" or "wrong" diminishes.

Mesonero's literary scholarship, then, makes up an abundant but secondary part of his work. As seen, these documents at times reveal important areas of his literary psychology. Several of his accomplishments, notably in the bibliography of Golden Age theater, surpassed anything available in his epoch. In accord with his Neoclassical training, Mesonero believed in the authority of the past and rarely departed significantly from the judgments of standard critics, especially L. F. de Moratín. A methodical moderation sets the tone for most of his work; nevertheless, he certainly deserves a place among the most productive critics of his day such as Alberto Lista, Agustín Durán, Martínez de la Rosa, Dionisio Solís, Manuel Silvela, and José de la Revilla.

III   *The Historical Writings*

Even though Mesonero was officially named chronicler of Madrid in 1864, his historical publications date back almost to his literary beginnings. Because these writings can only tangentially be considered "literary," they will be alluded to only in the briefest terms in order to fill in another aspect of Mesonero's life and work.

In a manner similar to his literary scholarship, Mesonero does not neatly separate his historical writings from his other interests. Many *costumbrista* essays begin with an extended historical introduction; also, long portions of the various editions of the *Manual of Madrid* and all of *Ancient Madrid* may be termed "historical." Likewise, Mesonero often published his original historical research in one of the journals with which he was associated, and then, in later years, either included a reelaboration of the same article in one of his book length works, or simply published it again in the press.

One of Mesonero's least successful pursuits was historical biography. Lacking are fresh approaches, new psychological or social insights, and the vigorous style which he commanded in other genres. Frequently his subject seems to function as a mechanism for certain favorite social or moral themes. As an example, we may cite an article entitled *El príncipe Alí Bey El Abbassi* (*The Prince Alí Bey El Abbassi*), first published in 1839 and reprinted in 1859 in an extended form.[9] Cast within an introduction which reiterates one of Mesonero's favorite themes —Spaniards often ignore their own famous sons in order to worship at the altar of foreign heroes—the immediate impact of the study itself is thus diminished.

Mesonero's affection for detail and anecdote is revealed via the text and footnotes of the above article and in others such as *Historia anecdótica. La minoría de Carlos II* (*Anecdotal History. The Years as a Minor of Carlos II*).[10] Don Ramón, having searched erudite documents, gave publicity in this study to little-known court intrigues of the seventeenth century.

The most curious of these works is a historical narration called *Antonio Pérez* which airs the sordid details of a murder and the following intrigue during the final decades of the reign of Phillip II.[11] This story easily could have been developed into a full length historical novel.

A related division of this material includes brief articles devoted to post mortem reviews of the achievements of many of Mesonero's colleagues who engaged in civic or literary activities. Manuel María de Goyri, the founder in 1822 of Madrid's first fire insurance society, is eulogized, as is Adolfo Rivadeneyra, son of the editor of the *Biblioteca de Autores Españoles* series.[12]

The most cultivated and best written portion of the historical writings are those studies dedicated to monuments and institutions of Madrid and the nearby environs. These essays include both descriptive and historical elements. Treated are such subjects as the Customs House, the *Buen Retiro* (a royal retreat), the city jail, and the Royal Armory.[13] In the article on the Customs House, the reader notes the same festive, lively style as that employed in the *costumbrista* sketches; Mesonero structures the building's description on a humorous but apt prolonged metaphor: the building's parts resemble those of a human body. Not spared are digestive and excretory comparisons. Other articles pursue the history of landmarks related to literary history: the city's monuments to Cervantes, the house in which Calderón died, the birthplace of L. F. de Moratín, the early nineteenth-century abode of Victor Hugo in Madrid, and many more.

CHAPTER 9

Summation

THE life and literature of Mesonero Romanos spanned most of the nineteenth century. He witnessed and participated in some of the most turbulent years in Spain's internal politics. Don Ramón's *costumbrista* sketches, his descriptive histories of Madrid, and his *Memoirs* attest to these events—although mostly in their effect upon Madrid's physical circumstance and upon the daily customs and attitudes of its people. Conspicuously absent from his descriptions is any emphasis upon the more visible events of public history. His accounts are human: they are scenic, not panoramic; the author stands beside, not above the players.

In a life and art which are tightly interrelated and offer little substantial evolution, it necessarily follows that one may speak of constants. Unifying the work of Mesonero is both a deep moral sense and a steadfast commitment to the betterment of Madrid. In a sense, each sketch is a chapter of a work which develops the capital of Spain as its protagonist. Mesonero served his city in his literature (through its entertainment value and moral instruction), and in his many social, economic, and even political efforts. Due to his early attainment of economic independence, Don Ramón's efforts appear today even more attractive, since he served without seeking further financial gain or public glory. Just as in his writings, his efforts for society seemed promoted from the chair of a second row observer.

The author of the *Scenes of Madrid* travelled to foreign countries and within Spain, but almost always in order to sharpen his powers of observation and to bring back new ideas for domestic improvement. The notion that he was a friend only of Spain—especially its past—and an enemy of foreign influences is patently false. In general terms, however, one may describe his attitude as cautious toward foreign moral influences but enthusiastic toward a new cosmopolitanism or urbaneness for Madrid. He also deeply admired technological improvements such as the modern railroad system of Belgium. If at times it appears that Don Ramon's attitude toward modernization and tradition is contradictory, it is only the contradiction inherent in an epoch of shifting, unstable values. The author's ambivalence reflects the deep social, economic, and ideological transformation then in progress.

Mesonero's art must be considered as a culmination, a creation, and a prophecy. As a *costumbrista* he participated in a form which at least owed its mentality (a spirit of observation and verbose, ironic humor) to the distant seventeenth century. Mesonero, along with Larra and Estébanez Calderón, crystallized a tendency into a form, into a new style. The vehicle was the periodical press. Nineteenth-century *costumbrismo* both commenced and reached an apex with these three. Of the group, Mesonero began first, presevered the longest, and did most to establish the definitive form of the Spanish sketch in later decades. A further aspect of his art as prophecy is the undeniable influence he wielded upon the coming Spanish novel of Realism. In previous pages I have alluded to the testimonies of Galdós, Pereda, and others in this respect. Alarcón also referred to Mesonero as a model. Montesinos has suggested that, among other things, Mesonero taught Spain's writers to see reality in a more direct manner; only the prior moral judgment continued to subjectivize Mesonero's prose.[1] Montesinos continues:

With all his defects, and they are many, and with qualities that we can suppose even superior in number and measure—especially if one takes into account his priority in the discovery of many types, themes, and motifs—the historical importance of Mesonero is considerable, and his influence, although diffuse, is profound and lasting. To Mesonero, more than to anyone, is owed the fact that so many subjects remained "in the air," saturating the literary atmosphere; therefore, when we find certain *costumbrista* themes converted later into a commonplace, we should first think of him as the initiator.[2]

Seco Serrano draws several original parallels which also illuminate the role of Don Ramón: "In *Ancient Madrid* Galdós schooled himself on Madrilenian life. The *Scenes* served as a stimulus for the novel of customs and the Realistic novel, from Trueba and Pereda to Alarcón and Galdós. The *Memoirs of a Septuagenarian* succeeded, in short, in marvelously completing the cycle of *National Episodes,* basic in the works of Galdós. Well may one say, then, that, in one way, the work of Mesonero, in its distinct phases, summarizes, in a very clear line, the literary trajectory of our nineteenth century, from Romanticism to the Generation of 1898."³

We must not, however, exaggerate the intrinsic merit of Mesonero's prose. Today its fundamental importance is as a historical record and as a conditioning factor for a greater art which was to follow. The sketch of manners as practiced in Spain by all except Larra was too diluted by a confused confluence of intentions, moral attitudes, and literary debts. There was little artistic intensity. Mesonero's own methodical equanimity and his emphasis on reasoned, and frequently discursive, didactic art also lessened his creative spark. Compared to those around him, Mesonero was, in his own times, an important, innovative writer. Today this vision must recede somewhat into a historical relativity.

Finally, some have viewed as proofs of Don Ramón's creative limitations his lack of success in poetry and drama, and his failure to produce short stories, a novel of customs, or a new series of sketches with a national focus. All of these things may be true, but in this study we have viewed enough positive accomplishments to more than compensate for his shortcomings. His life of social activism; his *Memoirs,* which are the most significant of those written in his century; his still unsurpassed historical-descriptive studies on Madrid; and his contributions to prose themes and style seem sufficient to assure his continuing place in the history of Spanish literature.

Notes and References

Chapter One

1. The *Memorias* as well as most of the major works of Mesonero may be most easily found today in *Obras de don Ramón de Mesonero Romanos,* 5 vols., ed. Carlos Seco Serrano, *Biblioteca de Autores Españoles,* vols. 199–203 (Madrid, 1967). Most references to Mesonero's work will correspond to this edition; volume and page numbers will be found in parentheses within the text.
2. *Trabajos no coleccionados,* ed. Sons of author (Madrid, 1905), II, 624.
3. Federico C. Sainz de Robles, Preliminary Study to *Escenas matritenses* (Madrid, 1956), p. 22; and Emilio Cotarelo y Mori, "Elogio biográfico de don Ramón de Mesonero Romanos," *Boletín de la Real Academia Española,* 12 (1925), 158.
4. Carlos Seco Serrano, Preliminary Study to *Obras* (Madrid, 1967), I, xvii.
5. Cotarelo, pp. 158–59.
6. *Trabajos no coleccionados,* II, 624.
7. Cotarelo, p. 160.
8. *Ibid.,* p. 163, n. 3.
9. *Catálogo de los libros que forman la biblioteca de don Ramón de Mesonero Romanos* (Madrid, 1875).
10. *Catálogo de los libros de la Biblioteca Municipal a su instalación en 1º de mayo de 1876* (Madrid, 1877).
11. "Galería de figuras de cera, X: Mesonero Romanos," *La Nación,* March 8, 1868, as cited in *Obras,* ed. Carlos Seco Serrano, I, lxx.

Chapter Two

1. José R. Lomba y Pedraja, *Costumbristas españoles de la primera mitad del siglo XIX* (Santander, 1932), p. 34.
2. José F. Montesinos, *Costumbrismo y novela* (Madrid, 1960), p. 34.
3. Margarita Ucelay Da Cal, *Los españoles pintados por sí mismos*

(1843–1844). Estudio de un género costumbrista (Mexico, 1951), p. 22.

4. E. Correa Calderón, Preliminary Study to *Costumbristas españoles* (Madrid, 1950–51), I, xii.

5. *Ibid.*, p. xiv.

6. *Ibid.*, p. xi.

7. A full discussion of this topic may be found in Clifford Marvin Montgomery, *Early Costumbrista Writers in Spain, 1750–1830* (Philadelphia, 1931).

8. *Ibid.*, p. 28.

9. M. E. Porter, "Eugenio de Tapia: A Forerunner of Mesonero Romanos," *Hispanic Review*, 8, no. 2 (1940), 145–46.

10. Ucelay Da Cal, p. 35.

11. *Ibid.*, p. 36.

12. F. W. Chandler, *The Literature of Roguery*, 2 vols. (Boston and New York: Houghton, Mifflin and Company, 1907); W. S. Hendrix, "Notes on Collections of Types, a Form of *Costumbrismo*," *Hispanic Review*, 1, no. 3 (1933), 208–21; and Ucelay Da Cal, see note 3 above.

13. Ucelay Da Cal, p. 49.

14. George Tyler Northrup, *An Introduction to Spanish Literature*, 3rd ed., revised by Nicholson B. Adams (Chicago: University of Chicago Press, 1960), p. 340.

15. As quoted in Ucelay Da Cal, p. 57, n. 118.

16. F. Courtney Tarr, "Romanticism in Spain and Spanish Romanticism: A Critical Survey," *Bulletin of Spanish Studies*, XVI, no. 61 (1939), 26.

17. Camille Pitollet, "Mesonero Romanos, costumbrista," *La España Moderna*, 15, no. 178 (1903), 46–47.

18. H. Chonon Berkowitz, "Mesonero's Indebtedness to Jouy," *PMLA*, 45 (1930), 553–72.

19. Tarr, p. 28.

20. See, for example, Juan E. Hartzenbusch, Prologue to *Escenas matritenses*, 5th ed. (Madrid, 1851), pp. i–ii; and A. Ferrer del Río, "D. Ramón Mesonero Romanos," *Galería de la literatura española* (Madrid, 1846), pp. 141–53.

21. Berkowitz, p. 555.

22. *Ibid.*, p. 565.

23. Mariano José de Larra, "Panorama matritense," in *Larra: artículos de crítica literaria y artística*, ed. José R. Lomba y Pedraja, Clásicos Castellanos, no. 52 (Madrid, 1960), 223–24.

24. Tarr, p. 29.

25. For a sample listing of some of these pamphlets, see Emilio Cotarelo y Mori, "Elogio biográfico de don Ramón de Mesonero Romanos," *Boletín de la Real Academia Española*, 12 (1925), 187–88.

26. Ucelay Da Cal, p. 42.

27. Prologue to *Panorama matritense*, in *Obras jocosas y satíricas del Curioso Parlante*, new ed. (Madrid, 1881), I, x.

Chapter Three

1. *Escenas matritenses*, 5th ed. (Madrid, 1851), p. 242, n. 30; also cited in Emilio Cotarelo y Mori, "Elogio biográfico de don Ramón de Mesonero Romanos," *Boletín de la Real Academia Española*, 12 (1925), 166–67.

2. *Trabajos no coleccionados* (Madrid, 1905), II, 553, n. 1.

3. *Ibid.*, p. 557.

4. *Ibid.*, p. 553.

5. *Ibid.*, p. 568.

6. *Ibid.*, p. 570.

7. Foulché-Delbosc, R., "Le modèle inavoué du *Panorama matritense* de Mesonero Romanos," *Revue Hispanique*, 48, no. 113 (1920), 257–310.

8. Matías Montes Huidobro, "Mesonero Romanos: el estilo como permanencia de lo efímero," *Hispania*, 52, no. 3 (1969), 402–403. The excellent discussion by Montes Huidobro partially concerns the perspectives from within or without Spain. In *Mis ratos perdidos*, a work which he does not treat, the discussion should revolve about the native versus nonnative Madrilenian.

Chapter Four

1. Carlos Seco Serrano, Preliminary Study to *Obras* (Madrid, 1967), I, lix.

2. Emilio Cotarelo y Mori, "Elogio biográfico de don Ramón de Mesonero Romanos," *Boletín de la Real Academia Española*, 12 (1925), 433–41.

3. Jean Sarrailh, "Le *Manual de Madrid* de Mesonero Romanos," *Revista de la Biblioteca, Archivo y Museo*, 2, no. 5 (1925), 159–64.

4. Seco Serrano, p. xxxiv.

5. *Apéndice al "Manual de Madrid"* (Madrid, 1835).

6. Cotarelo, p. 449.

7. Federico C. Sainz de Robles, Preliminary Study to *Escenas matritenses* (Madrid, 1956), p. 100.

8. Cotarelo, p. 451, n. 1.

9. *Trabajos no coleccionados*, ed. Sons of author (Madrid, 1903).
I, 5.
10. *Ibid.*, pp. 185–86.
11. *Ibid.*, pp. 75–92.

Chapter Five

1. *Obras jocosas y satíricas del Curioso Parlante*, new ed., 8 vols. (Madrid, 1881).

2. Having first appeared in 1835, this article is now usually included as the final sketch of the first series of the *Scenes of Madrid*. In my translation I have taken certain restricted liberties with the lengthy sentences and confusing punctuation in the interests of clarity. Wherever possible, I have attempted to retain the flavor of the original. I have used the edition of 1881 as cited in Note 1 above.

3. H. Chonon Berkowitz, "Ramón de Mesonero Romanos: A Study of his Costumbrista Essays" (Ph.D. dissertation, Cornell University, 1924).

4. A. Ferrer del Río, "D. Ramón Mesonero Romanos," *Galería de la literatura española* (Madrid, 1845), p. 145.

5. For the description of the one dimensional character, I am most indebted to E. M. Forster, *Aspects of the Novel* (New York, 1954), pp. 65–82.

6. Northrup Frye, *Anatomy of Criticism: Four Essays* (New York, 1960), p. 172.

7. Juan E. Hartzenbusch, Prologue to *Escenas matritenses*, 5th ed. (Madrid, 1851), p. ii.

8. José F. Montesinos, *Costumbrismo y novela* (Madrid, 1960), p. 58.

9. Hartzenbusch, p. ii.

Chapter Six

1. *Obras jocosas y satíricas del Curioso Parlante*, 4 vols. (Madrid, 1862). *Types, Groups and Outlines* occupies volumes 3 and 4.

2. Federico C. Sainz de Robles, Preliminary Study to *Escensas matritenses* (Madrid, 1956), p. 96.

3. José F. Montesinos, *Costumbrismo y novela* (Madrid, 1960), p. 52.

4. Emilio González López, *Historia de la literatura española: La edad moderna* (New York, 1965), p. 295.
p. 295.

Chapter Seven

1. *Cartas de Pérez Galdós a Mesonero Romanos,* ed. E. Varela Hervías (Madrid, 1943), pp. 35–36.
2. M. Núñez de Arenas, "Génesis de unas memorias. Una carta inédita de Mesonero Romanos," *Bulletin Hispanique,* 49 (1947), 395–99.
3. Carlos Seco Serrano, Preliminary Study to *Obras* (Madrid, 1967), I, xxv.
4. For a specialized treatment of the problem of memory in the *Memoirs,* see H. Chonon Berkowitz, "The Memory Element in Mesonero's *Memorias,*" *Romanic Review,* 21, no. 1 (1930), 42–48. In his study, Berkowitz casts a well-documented doubt upon many of Mesonero's claims for the power of his memory. This doubt does not, of course, demonstrate diminution of the work's historicity.
5. For example, E. Allison Peers leans on it heavily to document his well-known *The Romantic Movement in Spain,* 2 vols. (Cambridge: At the University Press, 1940), as do Martin A. S. Hume, *Modern Spain, 1788–1898* (London: T. F. Unwin, 1899) and V. G. Kiernan, *The Revolution of 1854 in Spanish History* (Oxford: At the Clarendon Press, 1966).
6. José Julio Perlado, Introduction to *Memorias de un setentón* (Madrid, 1961), I, 24.

Chapter Eight

1. *Trabajos no coleccionados,* ed. Sons of author (Madrid, 1905), II, 586–608.
2. In *Algo en prosa y en verso inédito,* ed. Sons of author (Madrid, 1883), pp. 11–18.
3. *Trabajos no coleccionados,* II, 426.
4. *Dramáticos contemporáneos de Lope de Vega,* 2 vols. (Madrid, 1857–58); *Dramáticos posteriores a Lope de Vega,* 2 vols. (Madrid, 1858–59); and *Comedias escogidas de don Francisco de Rojas Zorrilla* (Madrid, 1861).
5. *Tirso de Molina . . .* (Madrid, 1848).
6. *Ibid.,* p. 13.
7. *Algo en prosa y en verso inédito,* p. 27–41.
8. *Ibid.,* p. 30.
9. *Trabajos no coleccionados,* II, 463–71.
10. *Ibid.,* I, 444–75.
11. *Ibid.,* 407–29.
12. *Ibid.,* II, 492–97; 546–50.
13. *Ibid.,* I, 301–36.

Chapter Nine

1. José F. Montesinos, *Costumbrismo y novela* (Madrid, 1960), p. 58.

2. *Ibid.*, pp. 72–73.

3. Carlos Seco Serrano, Preliminary Study to *Obras* (Madrid, 1967), I, xcv.

Selected Bibliography

PRIMARY SOURCES

Since most of Mesonero's work first appeared piecemeal in newspapers, I will make no attempt to list the original place and date of these articles. Instead, I will list below the first and other major editions of the collections, dividing the material into those prepared by the author himself and those done by others. For a more complete reference—though not exhaustive in any case—to the individual articles, see the comments regarding bibliography given in Primary Sources, Section B, under *Escenas Matritenses*, edited by F. C. Sainz de Robles and in Secondary Sources under Emilio Cotarelo y Mori. The second volume of *Uncollected Works*, pages 639–53, also carries references to the original articles.

Besides those mentioned below, there are also a number of brief anthologies of the *Escenas matritenses* published in Spain, England, France, Germany, and the United States. These are meant for classroom use.

A. Major Editions by Mesonero Romanos:

Apéndice al "Manual de Madrid." Madrid: Tomás Jordán, 1835.
Artículos escogidos de las "Escenas matritenses." 2 vols. Madrid: Rivadeneyra, 1879.
Catálogo de los libros de la Biblioteca Municipal a su instalación en 1º de mayo de 1876. Madrid: Municipal, 1877.
Catálogo de los libros que forman la biblioteca de don Ramón de Mesonero Romanos. Madrid: D. R. P. Infante, 1875.
Comedias escogidas de don Francisco de Rojas Zorrilla. Ed. Ramón de Mesonero Romanos. Madrid: Rivadeneyra, 1861. Contains thirty plays.
Dramáticos contemporáneos de Lope de Vega. Ed. Ramón de Mesonero Romanos. 2 vols. Madrid: Rivadeneyra, 1857–58. Fifty-nine plays.
Dramáticos posteriores a Lope de Vega. Ed. Ramón de Mesonero Romanos. 2 vols. Madrid: Rivadeneyra, 1858–59. Sixty-five plays.

167

El antiguo Madrid. Paseos histórico-anecdóticos por las calles y casas de esta villa. Madrid: Mellado, 1861.

Escenas matritenses. 3rd ed. 4 vols. Madrid: Yenes, 1842.

Manual de Madrid. Descripción de la corte y de la villa. Madrid: Miguel de Burgos, 1831.

Marido joven y mujer vieja. Madrid: Miguel de Burgos, 1829.

Memoria explicativa del Plano general de mejoras. Madrid: Espinosa y Compañía, 1849.

Memorias de un setentón, natural y vecino de Madrid. Madrid: Oficinas de la Ilustración Española y Americana, 1880.

Mis ratos perdidos o ligero bosquejo de Madrid en 1820 y 1821. Madrid: E. Alvarez, 1822.

Obras jocosas y satíricas del Curioso Parlante. 4 vols. Madrid: Mellado, 1862. The first volume represents the initial bound publication of some new sketches written between 1843 and 1860, entitled *Tipos, grupos y bocetos de cuadros de costumbres.* The second volume includes *Recuerdos de viaje,* and the final two repeat the *Escenas matritenses.*

Obras jocosas y satíricas del Curioso Parlante. New ed. 8 vols. Madrid: Oficinas de la Ilustración Española y Americana, 1881. Last edition governed by the author. Included are all of the major collections of sketches, plus *El antiguo Madrid, Recuerdos de viaje, Memorias de un setentón,* and several new introductory prologues by Mesonero. Reproduced in 1925–26 by Biblioteca Renacimiento.

Ordenanzas de policía urbana y rural para la villa de Madrid y su término. Madrid: Yenes, 1847.

Panorama matritense. 3 vols. Madrid: Repullés, 1835–38.

Proyecto de mejoras generales de Madrid. Madrid: Agustín Espinosa, 1864.

Recuerdos de viaje por Francia y Bélgica en 1840 y 1841. Madrid: Miguel de Burgos, 1841.

Tirso de Molina. Cuentos, fábulas, descripciones, diálogos, máximas y apotegmas, epigramas y dichos agudos escogidos en sus obras, con un discurso crítico por don Ramón de Mesonero Romanos. Madrid: Mellado, 1848.

B.   Major Editions by Others:

Algo en prosa y en verso inédito. Ed. Sons of author. Madrid: A. Pérez Dubrull, 1883. Contains poetry, travel sketches, and the author's discourse of 1838 upon entering the Royal Spanish Academy.

Antología de Ramón de Mesonero Romanos. Ed. Octavio de Medeiros. Madrid: Editora Nacional, 1944. Samples of prose arranged by subject matter.

Costumbristas españoles. Ed. E. Correa Calderón. 2 vols. Madrid: Aguilar, 1950–51. Volume One contains several articles by Mesonero from each of his principal collections. Some perceptive comments about his art in the introductory essay.

El Madrid de Mesonero (Antología). Ed. José Hesse. Madrid: Taurus Ediciones, 1964. Excerpts arranged by their societal theme.

Escenas matritenses. Scènes de la vie de Madrid. Ed. F. Morère. Paris: Garnier, 1896. Useful for simplified introduction to author and his principal sketches.

Escenas matritenses. Ed. Ramón Gómez de la Serna. Buenos Aires: Espasa-Calpe, 1942. Introduction concentrates on interpretative biography.

Escenas matritenses. Ed. F. C. Sainz de Robles. Madrid: Aguilar, 1945. A useful bibliography concludes the lengthy but standard introduction. Includes *Tipos y caracteres.* Enlarged second edition in 1956.

Escenas matritenses. Ed. E. Correa Calderón. Madrid: Ediciones Anaya, 1964. Brief introduction and good selection of representative sketches.

Escenas matritenses. Ed. A. Cardona de Gilbert. Barcelona: Editorial Bruguera, 1967. A serious, well-written introduction with laudable emphasis given to style and techniques.

Memorias de un setentón. Ed. José Julio Perlado. 2 vols. Madrid: Publicaciones Españolas, 1961. Several useful comments in the introduction regarding structure and techniques.

Mesonero Romanos: estudio y antología. Ed. Mariano Sánchez de Palacios. Madrid: Compañía Bibliográfica Española, 1963. A schematic overview of the author's life and works, and a representative sampling of his prose and verse.

Obras de don Ramón de Mesonero Romanos. Ed. Carlos Seco Serrano. 5 vols. Madrid: Atlas, 1967. (Vols. 199–203 of *Biblioteca de Autores Españoles.*) Much useful and original thought in the prologue, especially with regard to the social plane of reality in Mesonero's sketches.

Selections from Mesonero Romanos. Ed. George Tyler Northrup. New York: Henry Holt and Company, 1913. Good selection for school reading; excellent introduction considering material available at the time of writing.

Trabajos no coleccionados. Ed. Sons of author. 2 vols. Madrid:

M. G. Hernández, 1903–05. Contains miscellaneous newspaper articles on such subjects as urban reform, education, description of places and monuments, literary history and criticism, biography. Also complete texts of all but one of the author's plays, some poetry, and numerous useful documents relative to the author's life and times.

C. Correspondence:

"Cartas de José Mᵃ de Pereda." Ed. E. Varela Hervías. *Bulletin Hispanique*, 60 (1958), 375–81. Seventeen letters which reveal Pereda's high esteem of Mesonero, and these writers' frequent exchanges of works and bibliographical information.

Cartas de Pérez Galdós a Mesonero Romanos. Ed. E. Varela Hervías. Madrid: Artes Gráficas Municipales, 1943. Twenty letters of biographical and literary interest.

"Cuatro cartas." Ed. E. Varela Hervías. *Clavileño*, 7, no. 40 (1956), 51–53. Letters from Alarcón, A. de Trueba, Pereda, and Cánovas del Castillo, all of which bear testimony to the encouragement that Mesonero gave to the younger generation.

"El archivo epistolar de don Ventura de la Vega." Ed. Pilar Lozano Guirao. *Revista de literatura*, 13, nos. 25–26 (1958), 121–72. Pages 142–44 carry three letters from Mesonero to Ventura de la Vega. They have more biographical than literary interest.

Núñez de Arenas, M. "Génesis de unas memorias. Una carta inédita de Mesonero Romanos." *Bulletin Hispanique*, 49 (1947), 395–99. A brief study of the origins of the *Memorias de un setentón*, especially as regards a possible stimulus by Patricio de la Escosura.

Cartas a Galdós. Ed. Soledad Ortega. Madrid: Revista de Occidente, 1964. Fourteen letters from Mesonero, pages 23–36, in which the latter's concern for the documentation of the *Episodios nacionales* is noteworthy.

SECONDARY SOURCES

The articles and other studies listed below have been selected for their critical importance as well as their availability. Brief newspaper articles, for example, which add nothing to our knowledge have been omitted. Also not included are standard discussions in the numerous manuals of literary history or in the works on the Romantic period. I have not repeated below the references given in Section B of Primary Sources to the introductory essays found in editions and anthologies of Mesonero's works. The most notable of these are by E. Correa Calderón, Carlos Seco Serrano, F. C. Sainz de Robles, A. Cardona de Gilbert, and G. T. Northrup.

As to bibliography, most of the anthologies given in Primary Sources carry brief but useful information at the conclusion of the introductory essay. However, only five bibliographies approach completeness, and reference to two of them may be found in the annotations below to the works of José Simón Díaz and E. Cotarelo y Mori. Also, volume two of *Uncollected Works*, pages 639–53, carries bibliographical material, as do the critical introductions of Seco Serrano and Sainz de Robles.

A. Books and theses:

Acta de la sesión y discursos pronunciados en la celebrada por la Sociedad Económica Matritense en honor de D. Ramón de Mesonero Romanos en el quinto aniversario de su fallecimiento. 30 de abril de 1887. Madrid: M. Tello, 1888. Typical eulogistic speeches by friends of the author.

BERKOWITZ, HYMAN CHONON. "Ramón de Mesonero Romanos: A Study of his Costumbrista Essays." Ph.D. dissertation, Cornell University, 1924. Some biographical information, but principally a highly critical view of Mesonero's art. Berkowitz doubts that Mesonero did more, in most cases, than transplant the Paris of Jouy to Madrid. The critic also denies the realism of Don Ramón's sketches; terms them "caricatures" of Madrid. Worth reading.

LÓPEZ ARROJO, SEBASTIÁN, ed. *Album en honor y recuerdo de don Ramón Mesonero Romanos.* Madrid: M. P. Montoya [1889]. Collection of miscellaneous writings, mostly unrelated to Mesonero, or highly sympathetic to him. A thoughtful comment by "Clarín" is the most meritorious contribution.

MACDONALD, ELIZABETH. "The Madrid of Mesonero Romanos." Master's thesis, University of Washington, 1924. A string of quotations in an attempt to prove that Mesonero dealt with all the important aspects of life in Madrid.

OLMEDILLA Y PUIG, JOAQUÍN. *Bosquejo biográfico del popular escritor de costumbres D. Ramón de Mesonero Romanos (El Curioso Parlante).* Madrid: M. G. Hernández, 1889. The first biography of Mesonero, but lacks structural clarity and objectivity. Very adjectival.

ROMERO, FEDERICO. *Mesonero Romanos: activista del madrileñismo.* Madrid: Instituto de Estudios Madrileños, 1968. Sympathetic treatment in a rather affected style, but full of important factual information. Fills a definite need.

B. Articles and Sections in Longer Works:

BAQUERO GOYANES, MARIANO. "Perspectivismo y crítica en Cadalso, Larra y Mesonero Romanos." In *Perspectivismo y contraste*, pp. 11–41. Madrid: Editorial Gredos, 1963. An excellent treatment of the interrelationships between authorial point of view and thematic vision in the *costumbrista* sketch.

BERKOWITZ, H. CHONON. "Galdós and Mesonero Romanos." *Romanic Review*, 23, no. 3 (1932), 201–205. Demonstrates through fragments of their correspondence and sketches that a genuine esteem existed between these two authors from as early as 1868.

————. "Mesonero's Indebtedness to Jouy." *PMLA*, 45 (1930), 553–72. Asserts strongly but inconclusively that Mesonero did little more than transplant the Paris of Jouy to Madrid.

————. "The Memory Element in Mesonero's *Memorias*." *Romanic Review*, 21, no. 1 (1930), 42–48. Traces all the references by Mesonero to his memory. Documents that there were other unadmitted sources for the *Memorias*.

BLANCO GARCÍA, P. FRANCISCO. "Los escritores de costumbres." In *La literatura española en el siglo XIX*, I, 328–48, 2nd ed. Madrid: Sáenz de Jubera hermanos, 1899. Insists that the festive irony of Mesonero is in sharp contrast to the mordacity of Larra.

CÁNOVAS DEL CASTILLO, A. *"El Solitario" y su tiempo*. 2 vols. Madrid: A. Pérez Dubrull, 1883. Strongly asserts the priority of Estébanez Calderón (the author's relative) over Mesonero and Larra. Maintains that *costumbrismo* arose partially because of the triteness, the overall failure, of Spanish Romanticism. In both cases, Cánovas' arguments can be challenged on the grounds of mistaken chronology.

CEJADOR Y FRAUCA, JULIO. "Ramón de Mesonero Romanos." In *Historia de la lengua y literatura castellana*, VII, 131–35. Madrid: Revista de Archivos, Bibl. y Museos, 1917. Biographical data combined with a vision of Mesonero as a writer of light irony who sought more the gray permanence of typicalness than the brighter but more transient colors of uniqueness.

CORREA CALDERÓN, A. "Análisis del cuadro de costumbres." *Revista de Ideas Estéticas*, 7 (1949), 65–72. Studies some of the techniques of which many *costumbristas* availed themselves, such as expressive, at times complex, titles; epigraphs; brevity; and reappearing character types.

————. "Los costumbristas españoles del siglo XIX." *Bulletin Hispanique*, 51 (1949), 291–316. One of the most orderly and convincing discussions to be found on the foreign and domestic literary sources of Spanish *costumbrismo*. Complete, but concise. This and the previous article have been incorporated into the excellent introduction to this author's anthology mentioned in Section B of Primary Sources.

COTARELO Y MORI, EMILIO. "Elogio biográfico de don Ramón de Mesonero Romanos." *Boletín de la Real Academia Española*, 12 (1925), 155–91, 309–43, 433–69. The study that set the groundwork for all following scholarly discussions on Mesonero. Still the best biography and the best bibliography of primary sources. Little analysis of texts.

FERRER DEL RÍO, A. "D. Ramón Mesonero Romanos." In *Galería de la literatura española*, pp. 141–53. Madrid: Mellado, 1846. An early biography, especially useful regarding Mesonero's public service record. Much more dependable than many of the nineteenth-century studies. Attempts some definitive statements on the author's temperament and character.

FOULCHÉ-DELBOSC, R. "Le modèle inavoué du *Panorama matritense* de Mesonero Romanos." *Revue Hispanique*, 48, no. 113 (1920), 257–310. Reproduces the entire text of Mesonero's *Mis ratos perdidos* after mistakenly accusing the author of plagiarizing from it for his *Escenas matritenses*.

HARTZENBUSCH, JUAN E. Prologue to *Escenas matritenses,* by Ramón de Mesonero Romanos. 5th ed. Madrid: Gaspar y Roig, 1851. A broad, very favorable discussion of Mesonero's prose. Astutely sees behind the apparent festivity of most of Mesonero's articles, recognizing their serious critical intent. First serious discussion of the style of "The Curious Chatterbox."

HENDRIX, W. S. "Notes on Collections of Types, a Form of *Costumbrismo*." *Hispanic Review*, 1, no. 3 (1933), 208–21. Traces Spain's *costumbrista* influence upon England—both directly and via France—late in the seventeenth century. Shows that Jouy imitated Addison and Steele, who, themselves, were inspired by such Spaniards as Quevedo and Guevara. Concentrates upon following the fortunes of early collections such as *Le livre des cent-et-un* and *Heads of the People or Portraits of the English,* and their legions of imitators.

————. "Notes on Jouy's Influence on Larra." *Romanic Review*, 11, no. 1 (1920), 37–45. Demonstrates that Larra at times borrowed heavily from Jouy. Also shows that Larra usually admitted his sources, soon learning to transform or greatly improve upon them.

LARRA, MARIANO JOSÉ DE. "Panorama matritense." Two articles published in *El Español*, 19 and 20 June, 1836. Reprinted in various later collections of Larra's work, including the previously cited (Chapter 2, note 23) *Larra: artículos de crítica literaria y artística* ed. José R. Lomba y Pedraja, Clásicos Castellanos, no. 52 (Madrid: Espasa-Calpe, 1960). First article is more remote, discussing the nature of an article of customs and its modern renaissance—especially in France. Stresses the inherent difficulty of combining philosophical observation with a brief, pleasing form. Larra bears witness to the truthfulness of Mesonero's sketches, a position which contrasts radically with Berkowitz' later remarks. Larra's only criticism is of Mesonero's style, which is, at times, too pale.

LOMBA Y PEDRAJA, JOSÉ R. *Costumbristas españoles de la primera mitad del siglo XIX.* Santander: Vda. de F. Fons, 1932. Reprint of an academic discourse at the University of Oviedo. Broad discussion of the three major *costumbristas,* including their precedents in the genre. Pages 34–35 deal with Mesonero, insisting primarily upon his "professionalism" in literature.

MARTÍNEZ RUIZ, JOSÉ. "Larra y Mesonero." In *Lecturas españolas,* pp. 89–92. Madrid: Espasa-Calpe, 1964. Sees Larra and Mesonero as together representing the literary society of their times: Larra, exalted and impulsive; Mesonero, calm, scrupulous, practical.

MOELLERING, WILLIAM. "Eugenio de Tapia and Mesonero Romanos." *Hispania,* 23, no. 3 (1940), 241–44. A brief rebuttal of Berkowitz' thesis that Mesonero was a slavish imitator of Jouy; finds, coincidentally with M. E. Porter, that Eugenio de Tapia is a legitimate source for several aspects of Mesonero's art.

MONTES HUIDOBRO, MATÍAS. "Mesonero Romanos: el estilo como permanencia de lo efímero." *Hispania,* 52, no. 3 (1969), 401–408. Using *El sombrerito y la mantilla* as a basic source, Montes Huidobro produces evidence that Mesonero employed a variety of techniques to attain the special ends of the sketch. Excellent study in that it does not begin with an a priori condemnation of Mesonero's limited purposes.

MONTESINOS, JOSÉ F. *Costumbrismo y novela.* Madrid: Editorial Castalia, 1960. Scattered references to Mesonero throughout, but special emphasis in Chapter 3. Recognizes Mesonero's "profound" and "lasting" but "diffuse" historical importance in the development of the novel. Many suggestions that his art suffered due to lack of stylistic vigor and "round," original characters. Seems disappointed that Mesonero did not pursue the short story or novel.

MONTGOMERY, CLIFFORD MARVIN. *Early Costumbrista Writers in Spain, 1750–1830.* Philadelphia: n. pub., 1931. A very illuminating study on the obscure publications and writers of the eighteenth century which provided a transition from Baroque to Romantic *costumbrismo*. Places the date 1750 on the origins of the modern sketch in Spain.

NAVAS-RUIZ, RICARDO. *El romanticismo español: historia y crítica.* Madrid: Ediciones Anaya, 1970. Pages 285–90 treat Mesonero. The critic seems to combatively confront Montesinos' disparagement of Mesonero's lack of willingness to be as aggressive and as satirical as Larra.

OCHOA, EUGENIO DE. "Mesonero (don Ramón de)." In *Apuntes para una biblioteca de escritores españoles contemporáneos en prosa y verso*, II, 340–72. Paris: Baudry, n.d. Traces for several pages Mesonero's biography to about 1840, and then reproduces several early articles.

PITOLLET, CAMILLE. "Mesonero Romanos, costumbrista." *La España Moderna*, 15, no. 178 (1903), 38–53. A Frenchman who writes sympathetically of Mesonero's art. A rambling, somewhat eulogistic article at the outset, becoming more of a serious study at the conclusion. Relates Mesonero to early French *costumbristas*, and signals the former's contributions to form and techniques.

PORTER, M. E. "Eugenio de Tapia: A Forerunner of Mesonero Romanos." *Hispanic Review*, 8, no. 2 (1940), 145–55. An important article which points to Eugenio de Tapia and his *El viaje de un curioso por Madrid* (1807) as a substantial literary influence on Mesonero's sketches.

REVILLA, MANUEL DE LA. "Don Ramón de Mesonero Romanos." *Revista Contemporánea*, 17 (1878), 495–502. Reprinted in *Obras*, pp. 35–42. Madrid: El Ateneo Científico, Literario y Artístico, 1883. Revilla focuses upon Mesonero's special brand of irony, his physical and psychological makeup, and his literary contributions to Spanish culture.

ROMERO MENDOZA, PEDRO. *Siete ensayos sobre el romanticismo español.* Cáceres: Servicios Culturales de la Excma. Diputación Provincial de Cáceres, 1960. II, 77–87. Touches rapidly upon most aspects of Mesonero's varied literary interests. Unique for a brief study in that it fixes upon the author's drama, literary criticism, poetry, etc.

SARRAILH, JEAN. "Le *Manual de Madrid* de Mesonero Romanos." *Revista de la Biblioteca, Archivo y Museo*, 2, no. 5 (1925), 159–64. After examining the public record, the writer is able to reconstruct the difficulties Mesonero had with the censors in publishing his *Manual de Madrid*.

SIMÓN DÍAZ, JOSÉ. *La investigación bibliográfica sobre temas españoles*. Monografías bibliográficas, no. 1. Madrid: Instituto de Estudios Madrileños, 1954. Uses Mesonero as the point of reference for a lesson in the bibliographical problems involved in writing biography in Spain. Many important references given as the "lesson" proceeds.

TARR, F. COURTNEY. "Romanticism in Spain and Spanish Romanticism: A Critical Survey." *Bulletin of Spanish Studies*, 16, no. 61 (1939), 3–37. Some incisive remarks about the principal *costumbristas* from time to time, but principally noteworthy for the distinction between an article and a sketch (*cuadro*) of customs.

UCELAY DA CAL, MARGARITA. *Los españoles pintados por sí mismos (1843–1844). Estudio de un género costumbrista*. Mexico: El colegio de México, 1951. Although direct references to Mesonero are sparse, this is an excellent source for background about *costumbrismo*. Historical development (foreign and domestic) and questions of style, structure, and purpose are intelligently presented.

VARELA, JOSÉ LUIS, ed. *El costumbrismo romántico*. Madrid: Editorial Magisterio Español, 1969. The introduction to this anthology suggests coincidental Realism and Romanticism in the nineteenth-century sketch of manners.

Index

Titles are given in the original language; in some cases, titles have been shortened to their most commonly known form. All editions of the *Manual de Madrid* are listed under this title. The works of Mesonero Romanos are grouped under his name. An asterisk indicates the name of a character in one of Mesonero's works.